CONTENTS

GW00367362

LIST OF FORMS

INTRODUCTION

The game of tennis is undergoing dramatic change from within and without. The United States Tennis Association (USTA) has proposed sweeping revisions in the way the sport is organized in the United States, changes that will affect not only professional players but also a child picking up a racket for the first time—and, of course, the parent introducing the youngster to the game.

Among the initiatives proposed by the USTA are expansion of its Schools Program, which introduces tennis to grammar school–age children and provides equipment to the schools and instruction to its participating teachers and students; revamping and revitalizing the National Junior Tennis League, hoping to develop a truly national Little League for tennis; eliminating national rankings for children competing in 12-and-under divisions, and thereby reducing early competitive pressure; and—for the upper echelons of elite junior players—creating a national coaching system that offers support and direction for the country's best.

How great would John McEnroe have been had he learned in his early teens how to tame the raging lion without putting out the fire?

Some of the USTA proposals reflect issues that we raised in *Net Results*, our first book. It focused on the need for tennis parents to be trained and is the companion to this workbook. In *Net Results*, we outlined some of the problems and issues facing tennis parents and suggested ways and means by which they could develop and sustain the proper emotional atmosphere in which their children could best succeed in competitive tennis.

Mental toughness training, we noted, is a critical element for both parents and children. We described the training as a special emphasis, in practice and off the court, on a player's emotional state as it relates to competition. Through visualization, through certain on-court rituals, through controlled breathing and the development of concentration under extreme physical stress, we pointed out that a player can develop mental toughness skills which could give him or her a significant advantage in competition. And, we stated, a player's parents can be crucially important in developing the proper atmosphere and support for this kind of training.

Parents regularly underestimate the stresses of a sport like tennis, with its country club, life-in-the-comfort-lane stereotypical image. Often they haven't played competitively; others are so highly focused on a particular goal—a ranking or a scholarship—that they neglect to notice the day-to-day pressure on their children. Many parents have bought the old saw that playing under pressure is *good*, that pressure in fact is the stimulus to a higher level of play.

That, as documented in Jim Loehr's *Mental Toughness Training For Sports*, is just not so. Top athletes, both professional and amateur, have described their peak performances as occurring in a pressure-free environment, where emotionally they are relaxed, confident, and capable of intense concentration, and physically, they are free of tension. This state we describe as the Ideal Performance State.

Mats Wilander demonstrates focus, relaxation, poise—all necessary ingredients for competitive success.

The strings are a neutral resting place for the eyes between points. Eye control brings emotional control.

Dr. Loehr, conducting research at Colorado's Center for Athletic Excellence, determined through extensive testing and interviews with professional and amateur athletes that much of the stress affecting the games of junior players was influenced by and intertwined with their parents. Coaches typically interpreted the anecdotal evidence they saw as meaning the parents were the players' problems and that the solution was to push the parents out of the way, out of the picture, out of the game.

That's not the solution. Parents must become part of the team, and they have to be trained for this role they're asked to play. For the most part, there have been no guidelines. Using their natural instincts—many, too many, want to embrace the late Vince Lombardi's homily, "Winning isn't everything; it's the only thing" —they go wrong far more often than they go right.

But ultimately the goals of the parents are the goals of the coach. They want their son or daughter to find fulfillment and happiness. That's why they get involved in the first place. For the coach to work effectively, he or she has to include the parents and give them roles to play. The coach has to be willing to give them feedback and regularly evaluate their performances, just as he or she would their child's.

In short, the coach—and, we'll see, the player—needs to train the parents to perform their roles and to teach them to be mentally tough. It takes emotional control to be the parent of an athlete, and it takes exceptional control to be the parent of an elite athlete. Regular discussion-and-feedback groups of parent, player, and coach are a cornerstone of this training.

To begin, player, parent, and coach must understand that without a three-way relationship, the player and the coach are simply not going to get together. The parents have to agree to be supportive and to use the tennis experience as a developmental tool for their youngster. As the primary support system, the parent must agree to provide transportation for the child to tournaments and practice, not to become overinvolved emotionally because of either the time or the financial commitment, and to mitigate both the on-court and off-court pressure the child feels by providing unconditional love and specific and strict guidelines on appropriate behavior. Cheating, our research indicates, is inevitably the parents' problem, the result of an obsessive need to win that has been fostered and encouraged at home.

Junior tennis, with its challenges and its problems, its pot-of-gold-at-the-end-of-the-rainbow allure and its burnout danger, often breeds high expectations. Parents must learn to tone them down and to tune them out. As they do, they'll offer their children the best chance for success.

The *Parent-Player Tennis Training Program* takes the theory and program outlined in *Net Results* to its next level: application. Through a system of team building, parent profiling, written agreements, stress management, problem solving, and mental toughness training, parents are brought to a new level of understanding and personal effectiveness with their child. The workbook takes parents into training. It is specifically designed to help parents perform better within the highly complex and confusing world of competitive junior tennis.

Jimmy Bollettieri's photographs help capture some of the common themes, feelings, and emotions inherent in the parent-player-coach triad.

THE PARENT-PLAYER TENNIS TRAINING PROGRAM SUMMARY

This training program consists of seven one-hour team sessions held weekly:

Session 1: The Team
Session 2: Profiling the Tennis Parent
Session 3: Putting It in Writing
Session 4: Dealing with Stress
Session 5: Problem Solving the Tough Issues
Session 6: Continuing Education
Session 7: Rules for Play

After the program is completed, team meetings are held either monthly or bimonthly.

The coach or teaching pro, the player, and both parents should attend all training sessions. The specific activities and procedures that make up each session are detailed in this workbook, which is essentially a team training manual. The coach is designated as the team leader. He or she is responsible for setting dates and times and ensuring that the sessions stay on track and are constructive. In special circumstances, where there is no coach on the team or where perhaps the parent is also the coach, one of the parents may have to assume a double role of parent and team leader. Parents should pay the pro his or her regular hourly lesson rate for the time spent in the training sessions.

There has to be an understanding between the parents and the coach that player training is, in part, parent training. Success on the court will be the result of lessons well learned by the player—and of lessons equally well learned by the parent. A committed parent has to recognize the need for ongoing training, and the committed pro has to recognize the need for giving such training. If all parties are working together, the outcome of competition will be to their advantage.

1

THE TEAM

Although elite tennis players have always had their own coaches, teams were uncommon until the concept was popularized by ''Team Navratilova'' in the mid- and late 1970s. Martina, who traveled with coach, therapist, and companion-confidante, revolutionized the conventional theory that the tennis player's career is a solitary one. And her success has led a generation of players to adopt the team technique.

The training program presented in this book builds on the belief that most young tennis players have the foundation for such a team within the structure of their families. Together, the parents, a coach or teaching pro, and the player can form an effective, functioning competitor—a sum greater than its individual members.

To create such a team, roles must be established; goals must be set; expectations must be measured in realistic terms; and all elements must be woven together in a structure that all team members can work within. There has to be mutual trust, respect, understanding, and common purpose. Team unity doesn't develop over-night. It requires time, patience, hard work, and dedication. The best players—the professionals—embrace practice. And that practice has to include emotional as well as physical training.

FIRST TEAM MEETING

In this team approach, meetings are held regularly. The first meeting ought to set up a structure on which subsequent ones are modeled.

The initial meeting should be scheduled by the coach and held shortly after the parents, coach, and player have begun their relationship. Obviously parents who are simply interested in their children's learning strokes need not be concerned with regular meetings. But parents of children who intend to compete—on vir-tually any level—ought to embark on such a schedule.

The discussion at this meeting ought to center on what roles each member of the team will play and on how those roles may evolve. A good way to begin is to review the reasons why the child is playing tennis and why it makes sense to step into competition.

Well, why *is* my child playing? you may ask yourself. Indeed, many parents —particularly those who haven't themselves been involved in the sport—wonder why they should support their child's interest in the game. Those who are deeply immersed may have forgotten what brought them to their level of involvement. So at the first meeting, consider that tennis serves the following purposes:

Parents need mental toughness just as sons and daughters do. It doesn't happen by accident. Parents need training too.

1. It builds self-confidence and self-esteem.
2. It teaches the child how to be a competitor and how to uphold standards of good sportsmanship and respect for opponents.
3. It teaches self-discipline and self-reliance.
4. It teaches goal setting and that hard work will lead to achievement.
5. It is a lifetime sport, good physical exercise, and fun.
6. It teaches stress management.
7. It teaches development of a positive attitude in spite of great difficulty and adversity.
8. It stresses problem solving under pressure. In fact, playing tennis can be perceived as nothing more than a continuous presentation of problems.
9. It teaches independence through travel and through relationships with a wide variety of people.
10. It potentially provides a route toward college. College tennis scholarships are more plentiful than ever, and college coaches are committed to recruiting. Successful players will get noticed.
11. It teaches emotional and physical balance. Tennis is proving to be one of the healthiest, least injury-prone sports youngsters can play. It fits the minimal requirements for aerobic fitness, and because of its integral nature, it teaches youngsters how to relax and how to recover under pressure.

Using these points as a starter topic, the parent, coach, and child can begin to define their roles. Once defined—and our recommendations on those definitions follow here—we suggest they be written down, dated, and signed by all members of the team. In a sense, this is the contract each team member is expected to abide by. (Forms for listing these roles are provided in this chapter.)

Finally, the parent, coach, and child—on separate sheets of paper—ought to write what they expect to achieve from the experience. What's in it for me? they should ask themselves as honestly as they can. Why am I doing this? When the goal statements are completed, the papers should be exchanged, read, and discussed. Then the final agreed-upon goals should be written on a sheet of paper that's kept with the workbook. (In fact, looseleaf notebooks for player, parent, and coach are useful accessories to this workbook.)

*The coach, the father, the agent:
Aaron Krickstein's team of Nick
Bollettieri, Herb Krickstein, and
Dick Dell. The message is "Keep the
pressure off."*

MEETING OUTLINE

1. Discuss current and future team roles.
2. Fill out role clarification forms.
3. Describe goals and expectations for the coming competition.
4. Read each other's goals and discuss them.
5. Refine and finalize the list of goals and expectations using the personal goal forms.
6. Schedule the next meeting.

This first meeting should take no more than an hour, with no more than 10 or 15 minutes allotted to each task.

OK, you say, but I'm still confused about the roles. How is the parent's different from the coach's? What is expected of the child? Who handles discipline? Who gives rewards?

These are complicated issues and may remain somewhat unresolved at first. Nevertheless, everyone should make an attempt to define them from the outset. Here is how we perceive the responsibilities in the ideal team structure:

RECOMMENDED PARENTS' ROLE

1. To be supportive financially and emotionally to the child and the pro.
2. To help the child constructively manage the competitive stress associated with junior tennis.
3. To assist the pro in gaining insights into and understandings of the child's personality and feelings.
4. To ensure that the junior tennis experience is a good one principally from the perspective of the developing person.

5. To be an enthusiastic and positive member of the team.
6. To make sure the child adheres to the principles of good sportsmanship and ethics.

RECOMMENDED COACH'S ROLE

1. To teach proper attitudes, discipline, and sportsmanship to the child.
2. To build self-confidence and self-esteem in the child.
3. To teach the physical and emotional skills necessary for success.
4. To educate parents as to what you are trying to accomplish and how they can help you.
5. In whatever way possible, to help the child achieve his or her goals in tennis.
6. To help the child understand what is necessary to accomplish these chosen goals.

RECOMMENDED PLAYER'S ROLE

1. To give the best effort possible—a full physical and mental effort toward reaching your goals.
2. To keep a positive attitude.
3. To communicate often with parents and coach regarding your feelings and frustrations.
4. To practice good sportsmanship and ethics above all else.
5. To set goals and work to accomplish them.

STEP 1

Let's begin by discussing each individual's role. Keep in mind that the roles will evolve, and that each person—the player, the parent, and the coach—will have to be somewhat flexible.

Some things you might consider as you start talking: understand that parents put their children on the road to success. Perhaps the coach or pro can cite examples; the parents may have role models they can recall. Even if they do not, it's clear from various research studies focusing on sports champions, children in sports, and adolescent behavior that by investing time and having fun themselves, the mother and father serve as powerful motivators for the competitive young athlete.

In this discussion, too, it must be acknowledged that as the child progresses in competition, the parents have to learn to step back in order for the team approach to function at its best. So if not at this first discussion then at later meetings, some of these questions ought to be raised: How does the parent take that step back? How does a motivator become a supporter? How can the child help to bring this role change about?

STEP 2

We've included forms for both parents to fill out at this session but, realistically, your team may include only one. If there are several children in the family, it may be difficult for both parents to be equally involved. If both parents work, only one may be able to make the sacrifice of time and interest. Or the child, the player, may be living with a single parent. If only one parent is actively involved, then that parent should fill out the forms here. But if two parents are part of the team—perhaps they intend to alternately come to team meetings, although we would discourage that—then both should fill out the role clarification forms.

Other members should complete the appropriate role clarification form—My Role as Coach [Parent, Player] on the Team—and sign and date it. It's our opinion that the more contractual the agreement is among team members, the less likely it is that inappropriate, destructive behavior will ruin the player's on-court chances.

STEP 3

Look at the tennis season ahead. The coach will be overseeing both the player's instruction and development, and tournament and/or league competition. What are each team member's expectations? To be ranked? To win a certain number of matches? To reach a certain level of play?

On blank sheets of paper, outline those goals. Each team member should make his own list. As you write, consider: parents will occasionally try to revive their own childhood aspiration for athletic glory, and children may compete not out of their own love for a game, but out of their sense that their parents will love them more if they do. Coaches may dream of greater fame and wealth if they can only produce the next sectional champ or young pro. Let's get it down now as to who wants what.

STEP 4

Now discuss the two lists each member has filled out—the roles, and the competitive goals. Do they seem to be in synch and complementary? Remember, communication is an integral part of any successful team, and you might as well begin now. Talk about every aspect of how the team will work in competition, and try to achieve a consensus of both the roles, and what those roles can be expected to achieve.

STEP 5

Fill out the following personal goal forms using the goals and expectations listed on your worksheets as rough drafts. On another sheet of paper, list the team's goals. These ought to reflect the level of competition sought, the time commitment agreed upon, and the amount of practice necessary. As with the other goal lists, we suggest you identify six stated goals, but you may want more, or fewer.

STEP 6

Schedule the second team meeting for the following week. Before the next meeting, we urge that parents read—or reread—chapters 1 and 2 of *Net Results*, our first book on training tennis parents. This workbook is designed as a companion to that book, and at the end of each week's outlined meeting and program, we'll identify a section of *Net Results* that's especially applicable.

Write out each component and sign and date this form at bottom.

My role is to:

I.

2.

3.

4.

5.

6.

Signature _____ **Date** _____

MY ROLE AS PLAYER ON THE TEAM

Write out each component and sign and date this form at bottom.

My role is to:

1.

2.

3.

4.

5.

6.

Signature _____ **Date** _____

Write out each component and sign and date this form at bottom.

My role is to:

1.

2.

3.

4.

5.

6.

Signature _____ **Date** _____

Write out each component and sign and date this form at bottom.

My role is to:

1.

2.

3.

4.

5.

6.

Signature _____ **Date** _____

What do you expect to get out of this relationship?
What are your goals and expectations?

1.

2.

3.

4.

5.

6.

What do you expect to get out of this tennis experience?
What are your goals and expectations?

1.

2.

3.

4.

5.

6.

What do you expect to get out of your child's tennis?
What are your goals and expectations?

1.

2.

3.

4.

5.

6.

What do you expect to get out of your child's tennis?
What are your goals and expectations?

1.

2.

3.

4.

5.

6.

PROFILING THE TENNIS PARENT

Competitive junior tennis can become a complex experience for parents who've never played the game at a high level. Tournaments are stressful, time-starved weekends, when children are often asked—if they're winning—to play to their physical limits. Rankings may be viewed as political, as well as competitive, results. Opponents can be precociously sophisticated in playing mind games across the net. The travel can be expensive and exhausting. Finding court time for practice, finding a sympathetic teaching pro, just finding the time to be a tennis parent …is it any wonder that many tennis parents are seen as overinvolved?

That overinvolvement, however, may be hamstringing a child's on-court success. In chapter 1, we outlined the structure for the team approach. In this chapter,

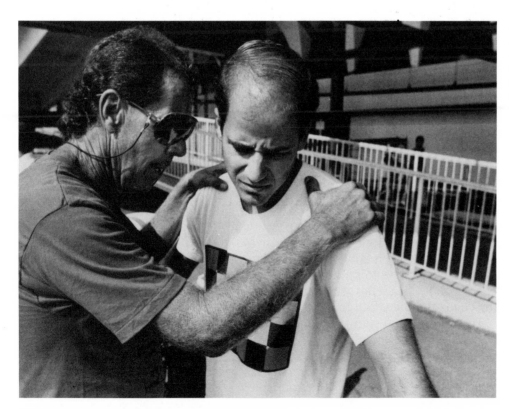

Coach Nick Bollettieri confers with Phil Agassi, who travels full time with his brother, Andre Agassi. Competition's pressure on family members can be as great as those on the player.

we focus on the team member most distant from the court yet the one whose performance is critical to long-term success. In *Net Results*, we reviewed some of the recent research that seeks to identify what makes a sports champion, an overachiever on the field of play. Inevitably parental support and encouragement, coupled with parents' refusal to stress winning and to punish losing, were the critical factors. Not being afraid to lose was a lesson champions repeatedly reflected upon as having learned from their mothers or fathers (and, equally inevitably, one or the other—but not both—played that teaching role). The sophisticated skills were learned later, from coaches. But the underlying mental toughness, the foundation for what we've come to identify through extensive interviews with athletes as the Ideal Performance State—that state of athletic excellence marked by fluidity, calmness, and complete attention to the task at hand—was planted early on and nurtured by these parents.

It's critical from the outset for both parents to identify their emotional strengths and weaknesses and for both coach and child to monitor parental attitudes toward competition. After all, the coach will see the child only a few hours a week at best. And the child will have difficulty separating what's happening on the tennis court from what happens at home. Parents rarely start out as problems. They don't have guidelines to follow, so their overinvolvement (a typical symptom is when the parent starts saying, "We have a big tournament this weekend") may appear to them an appropriate response to the situation.

Both overinvolvement and underinvolvement can be killers for the child. Honest feedback and communication are the best solutions, and on the following pages, you'll find a series of questionnaires for parents to fill out and for the parents, the child, and the coach to discuss.

These forms in a sense guarantee that the child isn't shortchanged in the relationship by not being heard. They give him or her an opportunity to evaluate his or her parents' performance actively rather than passively accepting their praise or criticism. Because the team approach is designed to develop mental toughness, which in turn will create better competitive skills, team members' work in answering these questionnaires honestly will be an exercise for them in mental toughness.

Understand that the questionnaire responses are not designed to cast blame or to criticize. Rather, they are intended to stimulate changes and new behavior. It may be an old saw, but it's true: self-awareness and understanding precede all significant personal change.

SECOND TEAM MEETING

Like the first team meeting, this one ought to be scheduled for roughly an hour. We have developed four profiles, including one in which the parents evaluate the coach. Team members may well decide to use, and discuss, only one, or two, or three of the questionnaires. That's OK. Any unused questionnaires ought to be saved for a later meeting as follow-up material. Obviously circumstances change, and team members ought to be evaluating themselves continually.

The fourth questionnaire, developed by coach Nick Bollettieri, is specifically aimed at the parent who is considering becoming his or her child's coach. Many parents have flirted with the idea; indeed, it's a rare parent who did not at least introduce his or her son or daughter to the sport. This questionnaire can provide considerable insight for the parent who thinks he or she can coach (or at least do as well as the pro hired). We recommend it as a kind of extra-credit exercise, after the team members have finished the first three.

What do you expect to gain from this exercise? We think of a properly involved parent as one who is balanced—at the midpoint, if you will, on a scale. An overinvolved parent can tip the balance to one side by becoming an additional source of pressure to win. Because of that pressure, a child's self-esteem—as we noted in *Net Results*—can be tied to performance on the court. The underinvolved parent tips the scale the other way, providing inadequate emotional, financial, and/or personal support. This parent gives little time or effort to the child's competition. The properly involved parent becomes a stable and enduring source of personal and emotional support. This investment of time, money, and energy is in no way tied to winning. The parent's principal perspective is the effect the tennis experience is having on the child's self-esteem and overall personal development.

If you, the parent, test out as a problem parent, a reevaluation of your role is in order. If your child is in the beginning stages of competition, then it's appropriate for you to be a motivator and somewhat involved. But once that atmosphere of enjoyment has been created, the motivation has to come from the child, the coach, and the child's peers. The necessity of a peer group of players shouldn't be underemphasized. Rarely—if ever—does a top competitor emerge from a vacuum. The rise of the tennis academy phenomenon, where players from across the country can gather to hit with others both their own age and ability level, demonstrates how peer group support can succeed at the highest levels. But at any level the parents' evolving role is to be an enthusiastic supporter from a distance.

In the best of all worlds, both parents will play active roles in the team structure. In reality, however, often only one parent will choose to do so. At this meeting, only one parent may be available to fill out questionnaires. Fine—as long as that's the parent playing the active role.

The coach may feel uncomfortable about filling out a questionnaire relating to the parent if he or she has had relatively little contact with the parent. Fine, too, as long as the coach then participates in the discussion. Most coaches ought to be able to describe what they are looking for from the parent and, from the responses on the questionnaires by both parent and child, ought to be able to conclude whether problems exist or may be on the horizon.

MEETING OUTLINE

1. Before the meeting, we suggest you read chapters 2 and 3 of *Net Results*. At the meeting's start, the parent(s) should fill out Parent Profile Questionnaires 1 and 2. Parent Profile Questionnaire 3 is designed for the player to fill out. Do all three if you have time, but try to spend no more than 15 or 20 minutes on them.

2. Compute the scores for each questionnaire and the combined composite score.

3. Discuss the composite result. Are the team members in agreement that it is a fair reflection of the parents' performance? Where, in the questionnaires' answers, did tough issues arise?

4. Draw up a list of the parents' strengths and weaknesses as outlined in the questionnaires and the discussion. Use the Parent Profile Summary Sheet.

Remember that the exercises in this meeting aren't intended to be an attack on anyone. Although the profile questionnaires may raise sensitive issues, discussions should be conducted within a constructive, optimistic, and frank but caring atmosphere.

Although we recommend that the tennis parent profile be completed in this second meeting, problems between parents and child or parents and coach may not emerge until later, even much later. Establishing this kind of dialogue now will create a basis for working out these difficulties. At the same time, reserving one profile questionnaire for later use can also be an effective tool.

STEP 1

Fill out Parent Profile Questionnaires 1–3 according to whether you are parent or player. Keep the exercise casual and informal. The more fun parents, players, and coaches can have at these meetings, the better the emotional nurturing of the player will be.

Parent Profile Questionnaire 4 is aimed at parents considering becoming their child's coach. Obviously that creates a different dynamic but with the same stresses and strains. This questionnaire is scored on a Yes/No basis, and —in our opinion —a single no ought to eliminate a parent as a coaching candidate for his or her offspring. The odds are weighted heavily against any parent-coach's being able to achieve the proper emotional balance. But, no doubt about it, it happens. Just ask Steffi Graf and her father or Jimmy Connors and his mother.

STEPS 2–4

Using the Parent Profile Summary Sheet, prepare a composite rating of the mother and father as tennis parents. Talk over the strengths and weaknesses the questionnaires described and highlight those on a list that the team completes jointly for each parent (if both are involved). Encourage all team members to discuss what they've seen and heard about other tennis parents—what they've liked, disliked, and would encourage or discourage. Remember that communication will be the backbone of an effective team.

The bottom line is that parents have to maintain an emotional equilibrium in order to help their children succeed competitively. That takes toughness and the ability to see one's role clearly. For parents, a crucial first step is understanding themselves and how they react under pressure.

Parents: Read the following statements and rank yourself using the following scale:

5 Always
4 Almost Always
3 Sometimes
2 Almost Never
1 Never

Then pass the completed form to the child and coach for them to score. Move on to Parent Questionnaire 2. Both parents should complete the questionnaire if possible, filling out the answers together.

1. Are you a source of additional pressure on your son or daughter? Is there pressure to win, pressure to be great, pressure to live up to your expectations? To what extent is your influence one of pressure?

   Score: _____

2. To what extent do you make your child feel guilty? Do you control your child out of guilt? You're spending time and money on him or her. What is the child doing for you? Is this the kind of attitude you have?

   Score: _____

3. Are you overinvolved (or underinvolved) in your child's tennis?

   Score: _____

4. Are you perceived by your child as supportive? encouraging? reinforcing?

   Score: _____

5. Are you understanding—sympathetic toward the problems and pressures of competition?

   Score: _____

6. Do you look relaxed, happy, determined, positively energized, and calm when your child plays badly or is losing? Does your son or daughter see this when he or she looks over at you?

   Score: _____

7. Following the match, do you show disappointment when your child doesn't live up to your performance expectations?

    Score: _____

8. Do you make the child feel valuable when he or she loses? Do you reinforce his or her self-esteem?

    Score: _____

9. Have you usurped the coach's role? Are you too involved in strategy or strokes?

    Score: _____

10. Are you overly critical?

    Score: _____

    How to score: Add the scores for all ten items together.

    Total score: _____

    Rating key: 10–20: Performing well
                       21–30: Slight problem
                       39+   Problem parent

Parents: Read the following statements and rank yourself using the following scale:

5 Always
4 Almost Always
3 Sometimes
2 Almost Never
1 Never

Then pass the completed form to the child and coach for them to score. Move on to Parent Questionnaire 2. Both parents should complete the questionnaire if possible, filling out the answers together.

1. Are you a source of additional pressure on your son or daughter? Is there pressure to win, pressure to be great, pressure to live up to your expectations? To what extent is your influence one of pressure?

   Score: _____

2. To what extent do you make your child feel guilty? Do you control your child out of guilt? You're spending time and money on him or her. What is the child doing for you? Is this the kind of attitude you have?

   Score: _____

3. Are you overinvolved (or underinvolved) in your child's tennis?

   Score: _____

4. Are you perceived by your child as supportive? encouraging? reinforcing?

   Score: _____

5. Are you understanding—sympathetic toward the problems and pressures of competition?

   Score: _____

6. Do you look relaxed, happy, determined, positively energized, and calm when your child plays badly or is losing? Does your son or daughter see this when he or she looks over at you?

   Score: _____

7. Following the match, do you show disappointment when your child doesn't live up to your performance expectations?

   Score: _____

8. Do you make the child feel valuable when he or she loses? Do you reinforce his or her self-esteem?

   Score: _____

9. Have you usurped the coach's role? Are you too involved in strategy or strokes?

   Score: _____

10. Are you overly critical?

    Score: _____

    How to score: Add the scores for all ten items together.

    Total score: _____

    Rating key: 10-20: Performing well
    21-30: Slight problem
    39+   Problem parent

Parents: Read the following statements and rank yourself using the following scale:

5 Always
4 Almost Always
3 Sometimes
2 Almost Never
1 Never

Then pass the completed form to the child and coach for them to score.
   Both parents should complete the questionnaire if possible.

As a parent, do you:

1. Say, "We're playing today," as if you were going to be on court too?

    Score: _____

2. Look disgusted on the sidelines when your child makes a stupid mistake?

    Score: _____

3. Treat your child differently when he or she loses, as opposed to wins?

    Score: _____

4. Withdraw love, affection, and warmth to get your child to try harder or do better?

    Score: _____

5. Feel your child owes you for all the time, money, and sacrifice you've made for his or her tennis?

    Score: _____

6. Look nervous on the sidelines?

    Score: _____

7. Get upset with your child when he or she loses?

    Score: _____

8. Walk away from a match because your child is doing badly?

    Score: _____

9. See your child cheat and do nothing or say nothing about it?

    Score: _____

10. Take notes or videotape tennis lessons?

    Score: _____

11. Let your child get away with foul or abusive language or racket throwing?

    Score: _____

12. Let your child treat the opponent with disrespect (not shaking hands at the end of the match or intimidating and accusing during play)?

    Score: _____

13. Allow your spouse to be a problem parent at times?

    Score: _____

14. Allow your child to treat you—or others—badly when he or she loses?

    Score: _____

15. Tie special privileges—perhaps a trip for ice cream, a movie, a private telephone, the use of the car, late hours—to winning in tennis?

    Score: _____

16. Place more importance on tennis than school work?

Score: _____

17. Find yourself frequently arguing with your child about tennis?

Score: _____

18. Spend too much time talking tennis with your child?

Score: _____

19. Consider the money you're spending a financial investment with an expected return?

Score: _____

20. Believe that were today the last day your child were ever to play tennis, the competitive experience he or she has had will have a negative effect on his or her future development?

Score: _____

21. Feel you're living out some of your unfulfilled needs or dreams through your child's tennis?

Score: _____

22. Get more upset than your child when he or she loses or doesn't play well?

Score: _____

23. Sense your child's tennis is more important to you than to your child?

Score: _____

24. Expect your child will become a successful professional player?

Score: _____

25. Suspect that other parents or tournament officials have viewed you as a problem parent?

Score: _____

26. Insist on accompanying your child to lessons and practice matches?

Score: _____

How to score: Add the scores for all 26 items.

Total score: _____

Rating key: 26-52: Performing well
53-78: Slight problem
79+ Problem parent

Parents: Read the following statements and rank yourself using the following scale:
5 Always
4 Almost Always
3 Sometimes
2 Almost Never
1 Never
Then pass the completed form to the child and coach for them to score.
  Both parents should complete the questionnaire if possible.

As a parent, do you:
1. Say, "We're playing today," as if you were going to be on court too?

   Score: _____

2. Look disgusted on the sidelines when your child makes a stupid mistake?

   Score: _____

3. Treat your child differently when he or she loses, as opposed to wins?

   Score: _____

4. Withdraw love, affection, and warmth to get your child to try harder or do better?

   Score: _____

5. Feel your child owes you for all the time, money, and sacrifice you've made for his or her tennis?

   Score: _____

6. Look nervous on the sidelines?

   Score: _____

7. Get upset with your child when he or she loses?

    Score: _____

8. Walk away from a match because your child is doing badly?

    Score: _____

9. See your child cheat and do nothing or say nothing about it?

    Score: _____

10. Take notes or videotape tennis lessons?

    Score: _____

11. Let your child get away with foul or abusive language or racket throwing?

    Score: _____

12. Let your child treat the opponent with disrespect (not shaking hands at the end of the match or intimidating and accusing during play)?

    Score: _____

13. Allow your spouse to be a problem parent at times?

    Score: _____

14. Allow your child to treat you—or others—badly when he or she loses?

    Score: _____

15. Tie special privileges—perhaps a trip for ice cream, a movie, a private telephone, the use of the car, late hours—to winning in tennis?

    Score: _____

16. Place more importance on tennis than school work?

     Score: _____

17. Find yourself frequently arguing with your child about tennis?

     Score: _____

18. Spend too much time talking tennis with your child?

     Score: _____

19. Consider the money you're spending a financial investment with an expected return?

     Score: _____

20. Believe that were today the last day your child were ever to play tennis, the competitive experience he or she has had will have a negative effect on his or her future development?

     Score: _____

21. Feel you're living out some of your unfulfilled needs or dreams through your child's tennis?

     Score: _____

22. Get more upset than your child when he or she loses or doesn't play well?

     Score: _____

23. Sense your child's tennis is more important to you than to your child?

     Score: _____

24. Expect your child will become a successful professional player?

     Score: _____

25.   Suspect that other parents or tournament officials have viewed you as a problem parent?

   Score: _____

26.   Insist on accompanying your child to lessons and practice matches?

   Score: _____

   How to score: Add the scores for all 26 items.

   Total score: _____

   Rating key: 26-52: Performing well
                       53-78: Slight problem
                       79+   Problem parent

Player: Read the following statements and rank each of your parents using the following scale:

5 Always
4 Almost Always
3 Sometimes
2 Almost Never
1 Never

My mother/father [circle one] is:

1. A source of pressure to win.

    Score: _____

2. Overinvolved in my tennis.

    Score: _____

3. Underinvolved in my tennis.

    Score: _____

4. Overly pushy about my tennis.

    Score: _____

5. Overly critical about my tennis.

    Score: _____

6. Shows negative emotion on the sidelines.

    Score: _____

7. Plays the coach's role too much.

   Score: _____

8. Uses the cold shoulder, or withdrawal of love or attention, to show disappointment with me and my tennis.

   Score: _____

9. Gets along very badly with other parents.

   Score: _____

10. Is nonsupportive with my losses or when things get tough.

    Score: _____

11. Is moody and irritable if I play badly.

    Score: _____

12. Communicates poorly with my coach.

    Score: _____

13. Always talks tennis.

    Score: _____

14. Thinks tennis is more important than I do.

    Score: _____

15. Is not tough enough on unsportsmanlike, abusive, or disruptive behavior or language.

Score: _____

How to score: Add the scores for all 15 items.

Mother self-evaluation score: _____

Father self-evaluation score: _____

Player evaluation score: _____

Rating key: 15-30: Performing well
                          31-45: Slight problem
                          45+   Problem parent

Another useful scoring method is to add all three evaluations together and divide by 3.

Composite for mother (average score) _____

Composite for father (average score) _____

Player: Read the following statements and rank each of your parents using the following scale:

5 Always
4 Almost Always
3 Sometimes
2 Almost Never
1 Never

My mother/father [circle one] is:

1. A source of pressure to win.

    Score: _____

2. Overinvolved in my tennis.

    Score: _____

3. Underinvolved in my tennis.

    Score: _____

4. Overly pushy about my tennis.

    Score: _____

5. Overly critical about my tennis.

    Score: _____

6. Shows negative emotion on the sidelines.

    Score: _____

7. Plays the coach's role too much.

    Score: _____

8. Uses the cold shoulder, or withdrawal of love or attention, to show disappointment with me and my tennis.

    Score: _____

9. Gets along very badly with other parents.

    Score: _____

10. Is nonsupportive with my losses or when things get tough.

    Score: _____

11. Is moody and irritable if I play badly.

    Score: _____

12. Communicates poorly with my coach.

    Score: _____

13. Always talks tennis.

    Score: _____

14. Thinks tennis is more important than I do.

    Score: _____

15. Is not tough enough on unsportsmanlike, abusive, or disruptive behavior or language.

Score: _____

How to score: Add the scores for all 15 items.

Mother self-evaluation score: _____

Father self-evaluation score: _____

Player evaluation score: _____

Rating key: 15-30: Performing well
                         31-45: Slight problem
                         45+   Problem parent

Another useful scoring method is to add all three evaluations together and divide by 3.

Composite for mother (average score) _____

Composite for father (average score) _____

Check Yes or No for each question.

1. Do you have a strong positive relationship with your child?

Yes _____   **No** _____

2. Have you been positive and supportive with your child in school and other activities?

Yes _____   **No** _____

3. Have you had good results in working with your child in other sports?

Yes _____   **No** _____

4. Does your child come to you when he or she has problems?

Yes _____   **No** _____

5. Are you able to relate to him or her when he or she needs support, and does your child listen and accept your advice?

Yes _____   **No** _____

6. Are you willing to make sacrifices for your child and, in turn, will your child make sacrifices for you?

Yes _____   **No** _____

7. Does your child respect your tennis knowledge and ability? Be honest in analyzing your tennis background. Do you know court strategy, drills, footwork, and conditioning?

Yes _____   **No** _____

8. Can you relate to your child in an objective manner?

    Yes _____ **No** _____

9. Do you have patience with your child? In your own profession, do you often resent having to follow orders? Do you blow up when business decisions take an unexpected turn for the worse? How do you normally respond outside tennis to problems? If you're a perfectionist, do you demand that from others? Are you intolerant of mistakes?

    Yes _____ **No** _____
    (If you are, you're likely to have problems teaching your child.)

10. Do you erupt when something's done by others that doesn't meet your expectations? Do you have a short fuse?

    Yes _____ **No** _____
    (Flexibility is a necessity in coaching.)

11. Are you willing to spend many extra hours with your child?

    Yes _____ **No** _____
    (Do you really have the time? How much time can you afford to spend away from your job and the rest of your family? How much free time are you willing to give up?)

12. Teaching one child makes others jealous. Animosity can develop. Are you prepared to deal with this?

    Yes _____ **No** _____

    How to score: Twelve "yes" answers may indicate an individual who can successfully combine parenting and coaching. Any no answers ought to raise a red flag against such an attempt.

Questionnaire 1

Score _____ Rating _____

Questionnaire 2

Score _____ Rating _____

Questionnaire 3

Score _____ Rating _____

Taking the responses given on the Parent Profile Questionnaires, list what team members believe are each parent's strengths and weaknesses. Do they keep pressure off? Are they overly critical? Are they supportive in losses? Do they put winning in perspective?

There may be fewer than six strengths and weaknesses. Don't feel pressured to make the list longer than team members feel comfortable with.

Mother's Strengths	**Father's Strengths**
1.	1.
2.	2.
3.	3.
4.	4.
5.	5.
6.	6.

Mother's Weaknesses

1.

2.

3.

4.

5.

6.

Father's Weaknesses

1.

2.

3.

4.

5.

6.

Before the third team meeting, we suggest you read chapter 4 of *Net Results*, which describes ways and means to introduce children to the sport. If the seeds of competition are sown properly, a great competitor will blossom.

The only real indicator of Boris Becker's greatness was his exceptional level of drive. As a young junior player, his passion to be great exceeded that of all his peers.

3

PUTTING IT IN WRITING (and other tools the child can use to help train the parent)

By now the team—parent, player, and pro—should have a sense of how the group can work together to communicate. With two meetings under their belts (or tucked into their shorts), the team ought to be ready to tackle some of the nuts-and-bolts issues of competition. Who's responsible for choosing and scheduling tournaments? Who brings the water jug? Who dictates when practices will be held? Each team member may have strong opinions on the most petty of issues —even which surface the child plays best on.

At this point, too, the team is getting used to working with paper and pencil. Now, we feel, is the time to begin to assess the responsibilities of each team member. You presumably understand the roles as they've been outlined in chapters 1 and 2. You also have a sense of how tough—as a parent—this junior tennis experience may become from the Parent Profile Questionnaires in chapter 2.

In this chapter, we'd like you to consider some basic do's and don'ts as they relate to the behavior and performance of each team member. We'd also like you to study together ways that the child can help to train his or her parents to become mentally tough and supportive but not overinvolved. The child cannot take a passive role in this team effort; both parent and pro have to help the player assert himself or herself.

Finally, we'd like all members of the team to conclude this meeting by signing a series of agreements. These agreements, which form the philosophical and technical backbone of the team, will help to formalize the team structure while making it clear to the child that a large measure of success will be his or her responsibility.

First, let's take a look at the do's and don'ts. Although we've divided them into categories for coach, for parent, and for player, it's important that every team member read all the lists. As with every other aspect of the team, information should be shared equally. Nothing ought to be withheld.

FOR THE COACH

DO:
Make your expectations regarding the child clear to the parents.
Meet regularly with parents and communicate your thoughts and concerns honestly.
Be supportive and encouraging but confident and firm with parents.

Tim Mayotte attended Stanford before embarking on a professional career in tennis. Pressures to turn pro early, skip college, and even finish high school by correspondence are real for many kids. Balancing tennis with education is crucial.

Be clear that parents must perform too.

Be firm and tough when parents get out of line.

Say at the beginning you will not work with a son or daughter unless the parents go into training as well.

Set performance goals for parents just as you would for players.

Understand that to coach young, developing players successfully in tennis, you must also coach the parents.

Keep your own perspective and emotional balance. When you're out of control, the team's mission quickly becomes impossible.

DON'T:

Tell parents that a son or daughter has the potential to be great if that potential isn't there.

Tell parents to stay out of the picture and leave everything to you.

Make winning the most important objective.

Consider all parents as impossible problems.

Forget that success in tennis is significantly correlated with a high degree of parental involvement.

Get into open conflicts with parents. Coaches rarely win in a struggle for power.

Neglect to communicate regularly with parents. They want and need your input.

Expect parental behavior to change overnight. Patience, persistence, and firm persuasion are the keys.

Get caught up in the fantasy that one of your students will make you rich and famous.

Neglect the team. The team approach is the path to progress.

Kalamazoo—"The zoo"—is considered the toughest junior competition of them all. One word sums it up—nerves!

FOR THE PARENT

DO:

Treat the child the same whether he or she wins or loses.

Try to have fun and enjoy tournaments and the travel. Your unhappiness can breed a child's guilt.

Look relaxed, calm, positive, and energized on the sidelines. Your attitude will help the child play better.

Make friends with other parents at tournaments. Socializing can make the events more fun.

Get involved if the child's behavior is unacceptable during match play. Your child doesn't want to be labeled a jerk.

Let the coach do the coaching. Too much input can confuse the child.

Understand that the child needs a break from tennis occasionally. It doesn't mean the child is quitting or burning out.

Be there when the child loses or gets discouraged. Be an understanding listener, not a fixer.

At the same time, give the child some space when he or she loses. Your youngster will want to be alone for a while, and then he or she will be OK.

Keep your sense of humor. When you laugh and have fun, your child's stress level takes a big drop.

DON'T:

Say, "We're playing today." Instead, say, "You're playing today."

Get too pushy.

Turn away when the child behaves in an unsportsmanlike manner on the court.

Tell the child what he or she did wrong right after a tough match.

Ask the child to talk with you immediately after a loss.

Make enemies with your child's opponent's parents during a match.

Act negatively and angrily on the sidelines unless your child's acting in an un-sportsmanlike manner.

Make your life your child's tennis.

Make your child feel guilty for all the time, money, and sacrifices you're making for his or her tennis.

Think of your child's tennis as an investment for which you expect a return.

Live out your own dreams through your child's tennis.

Try to take the coach's job away. Be the *parent*.

Compare your child's progress with that of other children.

Badger, harass, or use sarcasm to motivate your child.

Threaten or use fear to improve your child's tennis discipline.

FOR THE CHILD

DO:

Have patience with your parents; help them to understand when they mess up.

Give your best effort and work to have a good attitude. Otherwise your parents will have a tough time justifying their time and the money they're spending.

Give feedback to your parents on how you feel about your tennis. They want to know whether you feel stressed, whether you're getting along with your coach, and whether you're motivated.

Work on mental toughness. Make it an important part of the tennis effort, treating it as a life skill.

Have fun during the travel to and from tournaments. Tennis should bring you together with your parents.

Tell your parents if you feel they're putting pressure on you to win. A frank discussion will help maintain their perspective.

Understand that your parents won't let you become a tennis brat. When you get out of line, even if you've won a tournament, you're going to hear about it.

Understand that being a tennis parent is stressful too and that parents may be simply trying to do the best they can, even when they make mistakes.

Occasionally thank your parents for giving you the chance to play. It's nice for them to hear you appreciate their efforts.

Understand that their love has no connection to winning or losing. If that's not what you're sensing, let them know.

DON'T:

Treat your parents badly because you're under stress from your tennis.

Expect you have no responsibilities associated with all the money, time, and effort they're putting into your tennis.

Use them as scapegoats when you don't play well.

Treat them as slaves, demanding they fill your water jug, get your towel, fetch your balls, or grip your racket.

Keep them in the dark about your feelings about playing; talk to them.

Embarrass them by acting like a jerk on the court when things don't go your way.

Make them feel guilty because you believe they're not doing enough for you and your tennis.

Expect a parent to be able to read your mind when it comes to your tennis. If you want the parent to do, or not to do, certain things, speak up.

Practice with your parent and complain when the parent can't control the ball as well as your coach can.

Expect perfection from your parents. They won't expect it from you.

Manuela Maleeva's racket tells all: confusion, disappointment, low energy.

SOME OTHER TRAINING TIPS FOR THE CHILD

In addition to reading the previous lists, the team should study the following suggestions on how the junior player might collaborate in the training of his or her parents. The suggestions are designed to minimize the chance that parents will drift into overinvolvement.

1. Scheduling tournaments. The trap is to let parents do it all. To avoid that, plan well ahead. Get a schedule listing all tournaments in the coming year from the office of your sectional association. (For a complete list of the USTA sections in the United States, see page 134.) Then make an appointment with your coach or teaching pro.

Make out a tentative schedule of tournaments you want to play, choosing them relative to the ranking you've realistically aimed for. Once you and your coach have roughed out that schedule, take it to your parents for their input and approval. Put the final schedule on a tennis calendar where everyone, including your parents, can see it. The kitchen, for example, makes more sense than your bedroom.

Using a colored pen (red stands out best), mark the entry date for each tournament, and in another color (perhaps blue) mark the days each tournament runs. On the tennis calendar, too, mark any other appointment that relates to the game — lesson dates, team practices, practice matches, and so on.

Ask your parents to write entry fee checks for each tournament well in advance. Call (or write, if the distance is too great) the tournament officials for an entry fee form, and fill it out yourself if you can. If you need help, ask. But each entry form generally is similar. If you can fill out one, you can probably fill out all of them.

It's tempting to let your parents do all this work, but when you do that, you're opening the door for their overinvolvement. Parents feel that if they're doing the dirty work, they should be involved in the actual competition — and you don't want that. It takes time to prepare this kind of schedule, but it's worth it.

2. Equipment. Like scheduling, letting your parents take over gripping, preparing your water jug, or supplying clean towels is a trap. Instead make your own tournament list and place it where you can see it (here, your room makes good sense). This is simply a checklist of things to do (and have) prior to your first match. A typical list looks like this:

- Prepare water jug.
- Get rackets gripped properly. Have at least two or three rackets ready for a tournament.
- Get towels, extra shirt, socks, sunscreen, warmup suit.
- Pack medicine, if needed (for example, do you have asthma? Do you blister easily and need a blister kit?). Whatever your ailment, make sure you're prepared.
- Bring extra shoes.

Keep the clothing, medicine, shoes, and rackets in a tournament bag, and check the bag against the list. Make this ritual your responsibility, not your parents'. (Or a brother or sister, for that matter. In 1974 at the U.S. Open at Forest Hills, Chris Evert let her sister Jeannie be responsible for bringing her equipment bag from the Connecticut home where they were staying. Jeannie forgot the bag. And Chris — and Jeannie too — played in borrowed clothing.) You'll be training your parents that you don't need any help in these categories — and that will help them keep the distance they need.

3. Tournament watching. Suggest to your parents that they don't need to give you hand signals and that they don't need to show a disappointing eye or a frightening stare. Tell them to look as if they're enjoying themselves, and if they do get nervous, to fake a relaxed composure. "Just come and relax," say to them. If your play is off, if you're unhappy and losing, explain that you don't feel they have to stay and share your unhappiness. Tell them you've got no problem with their leaving to watch someone else's match.

But emphasize to them that they shouldn't just storm away when you're playing like a dog. If they want to watch, they should settle in, relax, and stay for the entire match. Tell them that.

Tell your parents not to clap when your opponent makes a mistake. Say, "I'd like for you to treat them the way you would treat me. And please do clap when my opponent hits a great shot. It's no problem for me, and I think it's important that my opponent recognize that I'm a decent guy and so are my parents."

Tell them not to make a fuss if they think you were cheated. You should handle that yourself, and their moaning and groaning — complaining that the ball was good, for example — isn't helpful. Tell them you'll take care of any problem and that if you think you're getting cheated, you'll call for a linesman. If one isn't available, explain that it's still your problem to deal with.

What about the parents of your opponent? Explain that they shouldn't be treated poorly either. Be friendly, and if they make unkind comments to your parents about you, insist that your parents ignore the comments. "They're not handling the pressure well," tell your parents; "they're not mentally tough." Say, "Don't sink to their level. I want you to be nice, to have a friendly relationship with the other parents. That's how I want you to perform."

4. Preparing Your Parents For Post-Match Distancing. Sometimes, after a match, your parents will be convinced that they knew exactly what went wrong if you lost. Before a tournament starts, remind them that, even if they're right, you won't want to hear that kind of analysis immediately after you've left the court. Explain to them that at that time you're not going to be listening, and you're likely to get upset.

Explain to your parents that you'd like to know what their toughts are—but not immediately after the match. If you played badly, you might say, "Mom and Dad, give me some space. Don't tell me right away. It doesn't work. All I'll do is get in an argument with you. Please give me at least 30 minutes to myself, and I'll be OK. Let me go scream, or throw my rackets in a field, or go cry, or whatever. Just give me some time to myself to pull myself together without having to talk to anyone. If you give me the 30 minutes and don't ask a lot of questions or tell me what I should or shouldn't have done, I won't behave like a jerk and treat you or anyone else badly. That's my deal. You just give me my space."

5. Prematch. Your parents may not recognize how important it is to you to arrive on time for your match. Emphasize that you want to arrive 15 to 20 minutes early. Tell them that you'll call to make certain the time of the match hasn't changed but that they have to get you there early.

Ask for quiet time before your match if you need it. Say that sometimes it's better for you to be alone, if that's the case. But explain to them what you're doing.

Parents often want to scout your opponent. Tell them, "If you have some thoughts about whom I'm playing, I'd be happy to hear them. Just don't make it too long, or too complicated before I play because it confuses me."

Tell your parents not to insist that you have to win, that pressure statements distract you. "Just do the best you can. Whatever happens is fine," is what you want to hear. Tell them that. Say, "Give me statements that take the pressure off, that make me feel that I'm OK whether I win or lose. Those are the comments I like to hear from you before my matches."

6. Cheating and unsportsmanlike behavior. Allowing your mother and father to let you get away with cheating or other unsportsmanlike behavior is as much of a trap as any of the other points we've listed. In the long run, you end up getting hurt. To train your parents to act as a check against this happening, set up criteria that will permit them to give you negative looks and comments and, if the behavior continues, to pull you off the court.

What criteria ought to be on this list? If you become abusive, if the language gets bad, if you chuck your racket—these kinds of behaviors. The list should be one you and your parents agree upon, and there should be consequences that extend beyond the moment: prohibiting you from playing tennis for a specific period. A severe penalty will usually cure you of the behavior. And you, in turn, are asking your parents not to let you become a tennis brat just because you're under the pressure of tournaments.

By setting up a system like this, you're telling your parents, "Although it's tempting for me to act out, I'd prefer that you make me aware of what I'm doing and that we set consequences for it."

Intensity, fight, and sportsmanship —the perfect combination. Yannick Noah is one of the best!

THIRD TEAM MEETING

Again, figure on an hour. Take some time prior to the meeting to look over the Do's and Don'ts lists, and have the child especially review our suggestions for how he or she might contribute to parental training.

By now, some tournament play will probably be completed. Certainly, all members of the team need a sense of how roles are being established and, in particular, whether the parent-child relationship is contributing to, or detracting from, the on-court performance.

By the conclusion of this meeting, the parent, the coach, and the child should have a clear sense of whether they're moving in the right direction, and whether the relationship is living up to the guidelines set for it.

MEETING OUTLINE

1. Prepare for the meeting by reading the Do's and Don'ts and suggestions on how a child can train the parent.

2. Begin the meeting by discussing the team's actual performance thus far.

3. Each parent should fill out the Role Change Form, and the youngster should fill out the Player Agreement Form. (Because it is important for the coach to stress to the parent the child's role in the training, we don't want that issue deflected by further discussion of the coach's role here, so there are no coach's forms for this meeting.)

4. Talk about the role change proposals, and then together, as a team, help the child fill out the Training Your Parent form. Make certain that the coach is comfortable with — in fact, *wants* — the child to assume whatever specific responsibility the child then lists on this form.

STEPS 1 AND 2

Plan to have read the Do's and Don'ts and the suggestions on how a child can train his or her parent listed at the beginning of this chapter prior to the start of the session. Then take a few minutes to discuss how those do's and don'ts apply to your team.

As we've often noted, it's easy to get caught up in the competition and its results and to lose sight of the process. Horror stories, such as we've noted in *Net Results*, of parents who've withheld privileges, who've even struck their children are, unfortunately, real. Use these steps as a period of reflection to make certain you're on track.

STEP 3

After talking about the do's and don'ts, each parent should fill out the Role Change Form, and the player should fill out the Player Agreement Form.

STEP 4

The Training Your Parent form is designed specifically for the player to use in training his or her parents. The coach's input is necessary here before anything is written down. How does the coach want to choose which tournaments to play? Does the coach agree and support the suggestions made? If not, why not?

End the meeting by filling out this form as a team.

Spacey racket, spacey concentration.

Things I will work to change

In general, I will _____

_____

_____

_____

_____

_____

_____

_____

_____

_____

Specifically, I *will do* the following: _____

_____

_____

_____

_____

_____

_____

_____

_____

_____

_____

_____

_____

_____

_____

_____

_____

_____

Specifically, I *will not* do the following:

1. _____

   _____

2. _____

   _____

3. _____

   _____

4. _____

   _____

5. _____

   _____

Signature _____ **Date** _____

Things I will work to change

In general, I will _____

_____
_____
_____
_____
_____
_____
_____
_____

Specifically, I *will do* the following: _____

_____
_____
_____
_____
_____
_____
_____
_____
_____
_____
_____
_____
_____
_____
_____
_____

Specifically, I *will not* do the following:

1. _____

   _____

2. _____

   _____

3. _____

   _____

4. _____

   _____

5. _____

   _____

Signature _____ **Date** _____

PLAYER AGREEMENT FORM

Things I agree to do:

1. _____

   _____

2. _____

   _____

3. _____

   _____

4. _____

   _____

5. _____

   _____

Things I agree not to do:

1. _____

   _____

2. _____

   _____

3. _____

   _____

4. _____

   _____

5. _____

   _____

Signature _____ **Date** _____

Things I now wish to take responsibility for:

1. _____

_____

2. _____

_____

3. _____

_____

4. _____

_____

5. _____

_____

6. _____

_____

7. _____

_____

8. _____

_____

Things I still want you (my parents) to do:

1. _____

_____

2. _____

_____

3. _____

_____

4. _____

_____

5. _____

_____

How I want you, my parents, to handle things (other parents, bad behavior, transportation, on the sidelines, etc.):

_____

_____

_____

_____

_____

_____

_____

_____

_____

_____

_____

_____

_____

_____

_____

_____

From childhood to adulthood. Parents either make or break the bridge.

4

DEALING WITH STRESS

This may be the most important chapter in this workbook. The relationship between training and stress and the connection between coping with stress and succeeding in competition is fundamental to our recommendation of the team approach to junior tennis.

The consequences of excessive stress in junior tennis are uniformly negative. Therefore its reduction becomes paramount in any effective training program. All training must include a stress cycle and a recovery cycle. A player who doesn't put himself or herself into stressful situations in practice won't be able to perform under stress in matches. Rest and relaxation, by the same token, are just as important as hard work and effort in the overall performance equation. In the end, training should include the appropriate stimulus, followed by an equally appropriate relaxation response, the recovery.

Using a system of reports, team members can monitor how well each is handling the stress of competition and its attendant commitment. The forms, and suggestions on how you might use them, follow. But first let's consider exactly what we mean by stress and how it shows up in performance.

Too often parents assume tennis begins and ends with stroking and strategy. But parents will inevitably face questions on stress once their children become involved in competitive tennis: Are the stresses of my child's tennis all negative? Or is there some good to be found too? Where does the harmful stress come from? Who is likely to be victimized? What are the signs that the stress is too much? What is burnout? Many of these difficult questions can be answered indirectly by better understanding the concepts of physical and emotional training.

Physical training is actually nothing more than controlled doses of physical stress. The principle of emotional training is exactly the same: controlled doses of emotional stress. The goal for both is progressively greater resistance to stress. Too much physical stress leads to physical breakdown: increased injuries, increased susceptibility to cold and flus (depressed immune system function), fatigue, decreased reaction time and speed of reflex, and overall reduced performance effectiveness.

Physical overtraining also has a negative impact on mental and emotional performance; the most pronounced effects are an inability to concentrate and decreased drive and motivation. Too much emotional stress leads to emotional breakdown, which quickly undermines physical performance factors as well. Signs of excessive emotional stress include decreased motivation, loss of confidence, increased moodiness and depression, increased temper and anger, increased negativism, irritability, and decreased enjoyment. Excessive emotional stress has also

69

Stefan Edberg at the ready. Rituals before serve and serve returns help to deepen concentration, stimulate appropriate relaxation, and raise intensity levels just prior to the start of the point.

been linked to increased risk of injury and a depressed immune system, just as with excessive physical stress.

The final stage of too much physical or emotional stress for too long is called *burnout*. It manifests itself most typically in a pervasive loss of interest and desire to continue the activity. In one sense, burnout can be interpreted as the body's protective solution to the problem of overstress. When athletes burn out, they remove themselves from the stress arena. It may well be linked to a primitive survival mechanism.

Proper physical training leads to higher levels of physical fitness, strength, and agility. The same is true emotionally. Proper emotional training, here referred to as mental toughness training, leads to increased emotional strength, control, and fitness. As a result of the training, the player has become more stress resistant.

It's important to understand also that the two training arenas are highly interdependent. Excessive physical stress will eventually cause a breakdown emotionally, and excessive emotional stress will eventually cause a breakdown physically.

An important distinction should be made here between *overload training* and *overtraining*. The overload training principle states that improvement occurs only

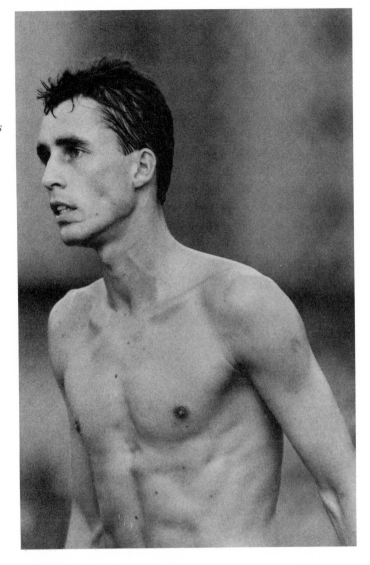

Mental toughness and physical fitness go hand in hand. Ivan Lendl is as tough and fit as they come.

when the workload is greater than that to which an individual is normally accustomed. The system—strength, power, circulorespiratory—must be challenged to improve. The person therefore must be pushed. The training stimulus or work required must progressively increase. Increased physical stress is a necessary precondition for better performance and stress adaptation. The danger comes with overtraining. Here the training stimulus (increased stress level) exceeds the body's adaptive capacity. The result is reduced effectiveness and function and ultimately breakdown.

These two flowcharts shown here outline the different effects of overtraining and overload training. Chart 1 diagrams physical training. It shows that overtraining, where the body is pushed too hard, leads through physical stress to injury. Overload training, on the other hand, teaches stress management without breaking down the body. The result is fewer injuries.

Chart 2, focusing on emotional training, indicates that overtraining for mental toughness—putting too much pressure on the young player during practice—

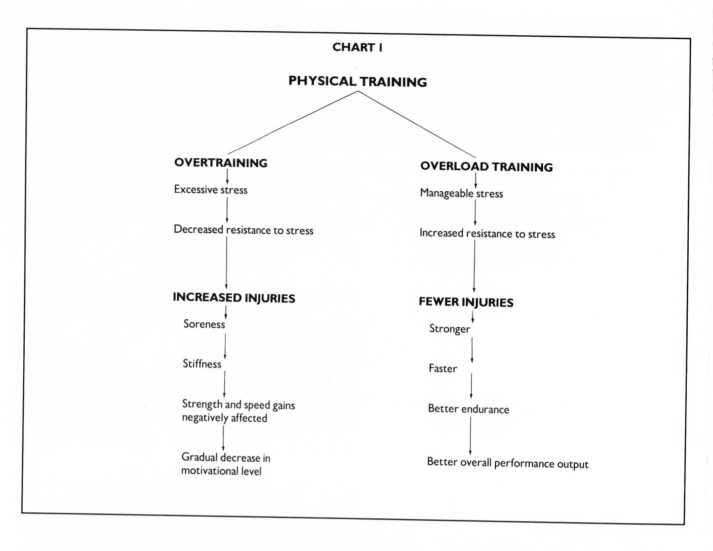

CHART I

PHYSICAL TRAINING

OVERTRAINING

Excessive stress

Decreased resistance to stress

INCREASED INJURIES

Soreness

Stiffness

Strength and speed gains
negatively affected

Gradual decrease in
motivational level

OVERLOAD TRAINING

Manageable stress

Increased resistance to stress

FEWER INJURIES

Stronger

Faster

Better endurance

Better overall performance output

could eventually result in the kind of short-tempered anxiety that can lead to burnout. Overload training, on the other hand, gives the child manageable stress in practice, and that develops the kind of emotional even keel that leaves the player resistant to bouts of temper and anger during match play.

Can any team member see signs of stress? Are there warning signals? Yes:

• Problems with sleep
• Irritability
• Loss of appetite
• Withdrawal from friends and family
• Loss of enthusiasm and energy
• General fatigue
• Moodiness
• Loss of sense of humor
• Quick to anger or temper
• Loss of motivation and drive
• Overly self-critical
• Lowered self-confidence
• Increased physical injuries
• More physical complaints (aches, pains, soreness)
• Concentration problems
• Increased frequency of colds and flus
• Confusion and disillusionment
• General apathy
• Uncharacteristic performance breakdowns

CHART 2

EMOTIONAL TRAINING
(Mental Toughness)

OVERTRAINING	OVERLOAD TRAINING
↓	↓
Excessive stress (biochemical)	Manageable stress
↓	↓
Decreased resistance to stress	Increased resistance to stress
↓	↓
Decreased drive	Able to sustain high positive energy levels in spite of crisis or problem conditions
↓	
Decreased enjoyment	↓
↓	Decreased moodiness during competition
Increased irritability	↓
↓	Reduced frequency of temper, anger, or tanking responses during play
Increased moodiness	
↓	
Increased temper and anger	
↓	
Decreased self-confidence	
↓	↓
Decreased Ideal Performance State control	Drive and enjoyment levels remain high in spite of adverse circumstances
↓	
Decreased problem-solving ability	

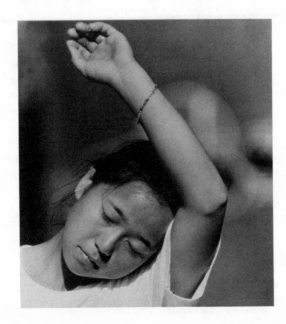

From the parents' perspective, it may look easy. From inside the player, it's a struggle that at times seems hopeless.

Martina Navratilova. Enjoying the journey is the only way to make the trip worth the price.

At its most basic, emotional stress is a biochemical response. It doesn't occur externally. A bad call, a gust of wind, or a tournament director who insists on a third match in one day isn't itself inherently stressful. Rather, it is a player's biochemical response that determines how stressful an event is. That, in turn, is determined by how a player has been taught—trained, if you will—to perceive the event. If the line call, or weather, or court time, or whatever else occurs is perceived as threatening, it will likely be very stressful. If the situation can be perceived as challenging, enjoyable, even fun, then little stress will be generated. Simply put, the more intense are the feelings of threat and anxiety, the greater is the emotional stress.

Two elements of this analysis are particularly important to parents and to the coaches of their children. The first is that an important part of emotional training is exposing young players to potentially threatening events and teaching them how to perceive and to respond emotionally to those events so the stress hormones are not dramatically triggered. The second is that the emotional cost of an event for a child can be determined by the degree of nervousness, anger, fear, depression, and negative or self-critical behavior stemming from the event. What may be extremely stressful for one child is not automatically stressful for all.

Burnout comes from too much stress, either physical or emotional. Working too long and too hard physically can produce it. So can too much psychological pressure. Playing too many tournaments in a row will frequently lead to temporary burnout: too many tournaments under too much pressure for too many years can result in permanent burnout. Burnout isn't limited to children. Year in and year out, top professionals complain of a circuit in operation 12 months a year. Regardless of the fact that the tennis season never stops, rest and recovery are fundamentally necessary to break the stress cycle. Chart 3, which lists the stages of burnout, can be used as a guide.

Evidence from burnout studies suggests that its effects accumulate in stages. In stage 1, the child's sense of enthusiasm and energy begin to decline. Young players will show more fatigue and irritability than normal. Early physical signs typically

```
┌────────────────────────────────────────────────────────────────────────┐
│                              CHART 3                                     │
│                                                                          │
│                         STAGES OF BURNOUT                                │
│                                                                          │
│                              COMMON SIGNS                                │
│           Stage 1           • Easily fatigued and irritated              │
│                             • Physical complaints                        │
│                             • Eating problems                            │
│                             • Self-esteem drops                          │
│                             • Increased moodiness                        │
│                             • Increased self-criticism                   │
│                             • Feeling of personal alienation             │
│                                                                          │
│           Stage 2           • Withdrawal                                 │
│                             • Self-directed anger                        │
│                             • Further decline of enjoyment               │
│                             • Severe fatigue and sleep problems          │
│                             • Sudden weight change                       │
│                             • Frequent and prolonged colds and flus      │
│                                                                          │
│           Stage 3           • Pervasive loss of confidence and self-esteem│
│                             • Intense depression and withdrawal          │
│                             • Serious lack of enthusiasm and energy       │
│                             • Virtually no fun is possible               │
│                             • Player is increasingly fragile and vulnerable│
│                             • Burnout                                    │
└────────────────────────────────────────────────────────────────────────┘
```

include complaints about upset stomachs, minor body aches and pains, and headaches. Eating too much, or not enough, is also associated with stage 1. As the young player's self-esteem begins to decline, the child feels increasingly less competent and is more self-critical. A sense of personal alienation begins to grow.

Stage 2 is characterized by withdrawal and anger—a quiet, passive, sullen, self-directed anger. Self-esteem, energy, and the sense of enjoyment decline. Prolonged colds and flu, severe fatigue, sleep difficulties, and sudden weight gain or loss are common physical symptoms.

The final stage of burnout is characterized by a pervasive loss of confidence and self-esteem accompanied by feelings of intense depression, alienation, and withdrawal. The player has virtually no energy, no enthusiasm, no fun with tennis and has real difficulty explaining why. Values can change, and the player is both fragile and vulnerable.

Who is most susceptible to burnout? Surprisingly it's often the children coaches most enjoy working with: those who are highly motivated, perfectionist, often overachieving, strongly influenced by powerful "oughts" and "shoulds," with strong needs to be liked, eager to please, sensitive to criticism, lacking in assertive interpersonal skills...kids who have difficulty saying no.

The pressure on children who leave home—and family and friends—to attend tennis academies face even greater stress than their peers who stay put. Data on stress examining three types of juniors—those at academies, those at home, and those attending academies but going home at night—show that full-time academy students are stressed by events off-court: lack of personal freedom, personal coaching, a scarcity of opportunities to have fun other than with tennis. Nonacademy students, working with a local pro, had stressors that were tennis related: not enough good people to play with, lack of progress, low confidence, and the level of their play. For the third group—academy students living at home—the greatest stress came from insufficient time. Balancing academy and school, and the travel from one to the other, left relatively little personal time.

FOURTH TEAM MEETING

Allocate an hour for this meeting. It will introduce the concept of monthly report cards for the entire team. We'll also recommend weekly reports from both coach and player to the parents, who can review them at their leisure. And we'll suggest that four times a year, the player grade his or her parents on their performance, using the criteria the team has established in the early meetings.

With the focus on stress and coping with it, the coach will be expected to contribute some analysis of the child's on-court behavior. In *Net Results*, we describe a charting system that breaks down the emotional peaks and valleys of a match just as a stroke chart does the strategic ups and downs. A coach, or parent, might consider coming into this meeting with the results of such charting for at least one match.

Now, too, parents and coach should attempt to create an atmosphere of peer reinforcement for the child's tennis if it isn't already present. Children are profoundly influenced by their peers. Simply to sign a youngster up for lessons, one-on-one with a pro, may result in near-instant boredom. A parent can provide powerful help by working with other parents to establish a primary network of friends who also play tennis at approximately the same level. Kids come up through the ranks in packs. Broadening a child's circle of friends so that he or she has buddies involved in the same activities means children can practice together, travel to tournaments together, and evaluate each other's games. A child who has no friends who play tennis and is asked to take the time to develop his or her game will resent time away from his or her group to develop tennis skills. It's a losing proposition.

For this meeting, we'll offer some questions on pressure traps that the player and coach should pose to the parent, and we'll ask the team to discuss various ways to manage junior stress. The parents, with the help of the child and coach, should then fill out the How Does Your Child Deal with Stress? form. Finally, the team should review the various stress report cards we've included and agree to fill them out for review on a regular basis, whether weekly, monthly, or quarterly.

MEETING OUTLINE

1. Read the introduction to this chapter. You should also consider reading chapter 3 of *Net Results*. Discuss how stress shows itself. Review the list of pressure traps (p. 77) and discuss them.
2. The parents fill out the How Does Your Child Deal with Stress? form. Coach and player contribute input.
3. The team reviews ways to manage junior stress. Discussion should center on how they can apply to the team.
4. The team reviews the report cards and agrees to fill them out on a regular basis.

STEP 1

We suggest you look at chapter 3 of *Net Results*. There, we describe the results of research that identifies the best emotional state for athletes in competition—the Ideal Performance State. It's characterized by superb focus on the task at hand coupled with a relaxed intensity that allows the competitor's skills to show themselves at their most efficient. Any external stress can diminish those skills and present obstacles to reaching the Ideal Performance State.

In this step, we ask the team to discuss the following pressure traps the parent can fall into, each of which will likely contribute to a young player's stress.

PRESSURE TRAPS

1. *Guilt pressure.* The parents should ask themselves: Do I motivate with guilt? Do I make my child feel guilty when he or she doesn't do well, saying that I've done so much for him or her?
2. *Investment pressure.* Do I expect a return on my investment? Do I suggest that to the child?
3. *Martyr pressure.* Do I think I'm giving up my happiness and life for the player?
4. *Pressure pressure.* Do I think that pressure is good for my child? Do I insist that even though I put a lot of pressure on my child to win, that is healthy? Do I think, "That's the way the world is. My son or daughter better get used to it now?" Do I *deliberately* put pressure on to win?
5. *Overidentification pressure.* Do I vicariously live out my life through my child's tennis? Am I satisfying my own needs? Do I imagine I'm on the court too?
6. *Family pride pressure.* Do I say that this is a family of great athletes, that there is a tradition of tennis—or other competitive—success?
7. *Self-esteem pressure.* Do I withdraw love, affection, and attention when my child does poorly or neglects to toe the line? Do I allow my child to feel good only when winning?

STEP 2

After talking about the pressure traps, the team ought to help the parent fill out the How Does Your Child Deal with Stress? form.

STEP 3

As a team, consider the following 10 ways to manage junior stress. Discuss how you can incorporate them into your program.

MANAGING JUNIOR STRESS

1. Be careful the child does not overtrain physically. Working too hard for too long increases the risk of burnout.
2. The child should practice for short periods of time with high intensity. Several short, intense periods of practice are better from a stress perspective than one long, enduring one.
3. The child should think of the time off between practice sessions or matches as part of training. Relaxation and recovery are as important as work and effort. Work to get the right balance of relaxation, fun, and hard work.
4. Do not let the child play too many tournaments in a row. How many is too many? That will depend on the child's age, stamina, and experience. The scheduling of bouts of emotional and physical stress is extremely important. If the tournaments are very stressful for the child, perhaps only one or two should be played without a break.
5. Know the stress signals. Ask the child to be aware of his or her stress gauge: loss of energy, moodiness, loss of sense of humor, sleep problems, persistent colds or pains, among others.
6. Help your child learn to say no. When the player has had enough, he or she should let you and the coach know.

78

7. Help the child take control. Situations are not stressful; people are. It's the child's *perception* of the bad line call, for example, that triggers the stress chemicals in the body, the biochemical reaction that distorts the fine motor skills needed in the game's strokes. Emphasize to the child that he or she is not a helpless victim; situations are challenges, not threats.

8. Help your child track stress levels daily. He or she can make a chart and rate the physical stress and emotional stress levels on a scale from 1 to 10. The closer to 10 in either category, the more important it is to relax.

9. Boredom is stressful. Help the child be creative in training. The best barometer of stress is how much fun the child is having.

10. Ask both yourself and your child, "If today was the last day she could ever play tennis, was it worth it?" If the answer is no, something is wrong. Don't postpone the child's happiness—or your own—until some special goal is achieved. The workouts and play should be enjoyable *now*! Only then is the price worth the payoff.

STEP 4

Examine the following Report Cards. As you know by now, consistent, accurate, and honest feedback is essential to ensure that the team remains functional and that both player and parents remain on track. There are four forms here: one for the entire team to fill out at a regular monthly meeting, weekly reports for player and coach to send along to the parents, and a four-times-a-year parents' report card that the player fills out, grading his or her mother or father (or both). It ought to be enough simply to read these over at this meeting and to talk about whether you want to use some, or all, at future meetings. Make certain you understand what they ask for and that you all agree on their importance.

The Weekly Coach's Report should be used by the coach to keep parents up to date on the child's on-court progress. It can be filled out in a few minutes at the end of the last practice of each week. The child can take it home.

At the end of the week's final practice, the youngster should fill out the Weekly Player Report (it should take only 5 to 10 minutes) and take it and the Weekly Coach's Report home.

Use the Monthly Team Evaluation Summary at all subsequent monthly team meetings. (If only one parent is active with the team, fill out only the appropriate parental column.) For the two stress-level grades, we recommend a low (L), medium (M), or high (H) evaluation. High stress or D or F grades for any member of the team ought to be the focus of this hour-long meeting's discussion. What isn't working? How can communication be shored up?

The Quarterly Parental Report Card is designed to provide important feedback to parents on their effectiveness in dealing with their child's competitive sports experience. Parents are performers too. If the competitive sports experience of young children is to be healthy and enriching, parents must perform.

Every three months, the child should fill out this form (a separate one for each parent) and submit it to the appropriate parent, with a copy to the coach. Then the parents and coach should meet to discuss the report card results. Make these reports a regular feature of future meetings. The trust you build among team members will pay off on the court.

Off-court: What are the signals that your child is experiencing greater than normal stress? Describe in detail.

On-court: What are the signals of stress on court for your child? Describe in detail.

Week Review For _____ **Date** _____

Attendance: No. of Days _____

ON COURT	EXCEL	FAIR	POOR
Attitude			
Effort			
Progress			
Respect to staff			
Stress level	L	M	H

Comments: _____

_____

_____

_____

_____

_____

_____

_____

_____

_____

_____

_____

_____

_____

_____

_____

Coach

Name _____ **Date** _____

Each of the following items should be answered according to what happened during the past seven days.

1.	Motivation to play tennis	1 Low	2	3	4	5 High
2.	Enjoyment of your tennis	1 Low	2	3	4	5 High
3.	Confidence this week	1 Low	2	3	4	5 High
4.	Pressure and stress this week	1 Low	2	3	4	5 High
5.	Attitude this week	1 Poor	2	3	4	5 Great
6.	Emotional control	1 Poor	2	3	4	5 Great
7.	How hard did you work this week?	1 Easy	2	3	4	5 Very Hard
8.	How much sleep this week?	1 Little	2	3	4	5 A Lot
9.	How was your diet this week?	1 Poor	2	3	4	5 Great
10.	How well did you play?	1 Poor	2	3	4	5 Great

Any special circumstances this week (injuries, school pressures, tournament week, etc.):

_____

_____

_____

_____

Month _____

Year _____

Player's Evaluation of Parents

	MOTHER	FATHER
Healthy interest		
No pressure		
Supportive		
No guilt		
Positive attitude		
Helps emotionally		
Not overinvolved		
Relaxed on the sidelines		
Doesn't coach		
Doesn't talk tennis too much		
Overall evaluation		

Parent's Evaluation of Player

	MOTHER	FATHER
Sportsmanship		
Attitude (tennis)		
Communication with parents about tennis		
Schoolwork		
Following overall plan		
Overall evaluation		
Stress level	L M H	

Coach's Evaluation of Parents

	MOTHER	FATHER
Healthy interest		
No pressure		
Supportive		
Positive attitude		
Not overinvolved		
Doesn't coach		
Good communication		
Following overall plan		
Overall evaluation		

Coach's Evaluation of Player

	GRADE
Effort	
Attitude	
Sportsmanship	
Discipline	
Responsibility	
Mental toughness	
Progress	
Following overall plan	
Overall evaluation	
Stress level	L M H

A—Excellent   B—Good   C—Average   D—Poor   F—Failure
L—Low   M—Medium   H—High

Comments: _____

_____

_____

Parent's Name _____

Player's Name _____

Reporting Period _____

Grading categories:
A Excellent performance
B Good performance
C Average performance
D Poor performance
F Failure

Parent shares a healthy interest in my tennis _____

Parent doesn't put pressure on me to win _____

Parent is supportive and encouraging about my tennis _____

Parent doesn't make me feel guilty about the money and time being spent on my tennis _____

Parent has a positive attitude about my tennis _____

Parent helps me emotionally when I have hard or difficult times in my tennis _____

Parent is not getting overinvolved in my tennis _____

Parent looks very positive and relaxed during my matches _____

Parent doesn't try to be my coach but lets my pro do that _____

Parent doesn't nag me for failure to play more tennis, do my exercises, running, and so forth _____

Parent helps me to feel good about myself and my tennis _____

Overall evaluation as a tennis parent _____

Suggestions: _____

_____

_____

_____

Signature _____ **Date** _____

Parent's Name _____

Player's Name _____

Reporting Period _____

Grading categories:

A Excellent performance
B Good performance
C Average performance
D Poor performance
F Failure

Parent shares a healthy interest in my tennis _____

Parent doesn't put pressure on me to win _____

Parent is supportive and encouraging about my tennis _____

Parent doesn't make me feel guilty about the money and time being spent on my tennis _____

Parent has a positive attitude about my tennis _____

Parent helps me emotionally when I have hard or difficult times in my tennis _____

Parent is not getting overinvolved in my tennis _____

Parent looks very positive and relaxed during my matches _____

Parent doesn't try to be my coach but lets my pro do that _____

Parent doesn't nag me for failure to play more tennis, do my exercises, running and so forth _____

Parent helps me to feel good about myself and my tennis _____

Overall evaluation as a tennis parent _____

Suggestions: _____

_____

_____

_____

Signature _____ **Date** _____

PROBLEM SOLVING THE TOUGH ISSUES

Some parents have had athletic experience at the high school varsity level, fewer at college, and only the smallest fraction have competed professionally. Yet many presume to understand the complexity of athletic competition, even when their personal experience begs to differ. For junior tennis players and their parents, the potential for misunderstanding is equally great.

Because many tennis parents find themselves immersed in a sport at a level far beyond any competition they themselves played, situations arise with which they're ill equipped to cope. This adds to the stress their son or daughter is trying to handle.

There are a variety of tough issues that parents must confront. In this chapter, we'll outline them and offer some detailed suggestions on coping with each.

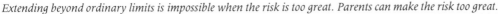

Extending beyond ordinary limits is impossible when the risk is too great. Parents can make the risk too great.

FIFTH TEAM MEETING

Allocate an hour or so. The focus of this meeting will be the 29 scenarios outlined in the following pages and how they may or may not apply to your junior tennis experience. Don't worry about gender identification. We've used *male* or *female*, *son* or *daughter*, pretty much interchangeably. If the scenario fits except for gender, then it fits.

MEETING OUTLINE

1. Examine the 29 questions on the Which Should We Discuss? form. Ask yourselves which apply to your team and which don't. Reading them aloud may be the best way to do this. For the ones that *do* apply, circle "yes" (correspondingly, for the ones that don't, circle "no").

2. On the Toughest Issues form, each member of the team should list the tough issues as he or she sees them. Use this page for any additional issues you've identified.

3. Solve the tough issues through discussion. We have provided some comments on each of the 29 issues, starting on page 99. Refer to them as you wish.

STEP 1

The 29 toughest issues we've identified through our junior tennis experience appear on the What Should We Discuss? form. They run the gamut from problems a beginning competitor may face to situations confronted well up the competitive junior tennis ladder. Read them carefully. Also feel free to add your own tough issues to the form.

STEP 2

Fill out the Our Toughest Issues form. Encourage each member of the team to be honest and forthright about the problems he or she sees.

STEP 3

Use the rest of the meeting to solve problems. We've included our comments on the 29 issues listed in What Should We Discuss? You might refer to the specific comments on the issues your team focuses upon, or you may want to read all 29 comments for a comprehensive overview of the problem-solving approach.

		YES	NO
1.	My child doesn't want me to watch his matches. Must I comply? See p. 99	___	___
2.	My daughter shows great promise, but we don't have the money to pay for the kinds of lessons and the travel necessary, as far as we're concerned, for her to reach her full potential. Our only alternative would be to take a second mortgage on our home. Would you advise us to do that? See p. 100	___	___
3.	My son swears and throws his racket during matches and even—on occasion—during practice. What would you suggest we do? See p. 100	___	___
4.	Our daughter's been playing tennis for nearly five years and has not been doing as well as she'd hoped she'd be able to do. She's just told us she'd like to quit. Should we let her? See p. 100	___	___
5.	Our son likes his coach very much, but both my husband and I feel he's a poor coach. What should we do? See p. 101	___	___
6.	Our daughter has decided she wants to go to a tennis academy away from home. She's only 14. Should we allow her to go? See p. 101	___	___
7.	How do we know if the stress levels are too high for our daughter? She's very sensitive and keeps everything inside. What are the signals? See p. 102	___	___
8.	My son treats me badly when he's not playing well, particularly after he loses. In fact, he treats everyone badly after a loss! Should we accept this as a difficult time and allow it to occur? What can we do? See p. 102	___	___
9.	Our daughter is not mentally tough, and there are no pros in our area who teach mental toughness training. What would you recommend? See p. 103	___	___
10.	Our son is very talented and does well in a number of sports. He's 13 years old and doesn't want to specialize. He likes to play soccer, basketball, and tennis and runs track too. Should we let him play all the sports, or should we get him to focus on one so he will achieve enough skill to be successful? See p. 103	___	___
11.	Our daughter is terribly afraid to play tournaments. She loves to take lessons and loves to hit, but as soon as we suggest a tournament, she freezes. Should we force her to play a few so that she can overcome this, or should we let it go? See p. 103	___	___
12.	Our daughter wants to play every tournament that comes up. Should we let her? See p. 103	___	___

		YES	NO

13. Our daughter can't stand to talk about her tennis with us. Every time we bring it up, she gets defensive. What can we do? See p. 104

14. Our son is constantly injured. Every time he gets going, he's injured again. It's hard on him emotionally. What can we do? See p. 105

15. Our daughter has unrealistic goals. Should we let her pursue them or force her to lower her expectations? See p. 105

16. Our son has no discipline in his training. He wants to be good but is inconsistent and irresponsible about arranging for court time, scheduling lessons, and finding practice partners. What should we do? See p. 106

17. Our daughter is doing poorly in school. Should we take away tennis as a punishment? See p. 106

18. Is it right for our family to give up vacations and other personal time for our son's tennis? We find ourselves constantly changing our plans to coincide with his tournament schedule. Is that appropriate? See p. 106

19. I see so many young children who've become tennis brats. How does that happen? How can I prevent it from happening to my own kids? See p. 106

20. My son always wants to play sets. When I win—and I'm the better player— he goes crazy. Should I purposely lose to give him confidence? See p. 107

21. I am a teaching pro who teaches her own children. Can that work? The expense of hiring someone else is too great, and there's no one else nearby anyway. See p. 108

22. My daughter's 11 years old, and all she wants to do is play tennis. She'd play 10 hours a day if I let her. Is it bad to let her play as much as she likes? See p. 108

23. Are there any personality patterns that seem to be a higher risk for burnout than others? See p. 108

24. Is there anything I can do constructively while I watch lessons and matches? Can I take notes or tape videos, for example? See p. 109

25. When should my son travel with a coach? Is it okay that I fill that role if a coach cannot travel? What are the pros and cons? See p. 110

		YES	NO

26. How much school should I allow my son or daughter to miss? There always seems to be a tournament that conflicts with academic time. Should tennis be elevated to the same level of importance as school? See p. 110   _____   _____

27. Should I do all the dirty work? Fetch drinks, towels, regrip rackets, prepare meals, do the laundry, arrange for transportation—who should do all the little things like this? Is that part of the parental role? See p. 111   _____   _____

28. Should I set up matches—call people for my daughter—until she learns to do it herself? See p. 111   _____   _____

29. It's a real sacrifice for us to pay for all the lessons and clinics. Our son isn't trying; he's not giving his best effort. He shows up late, doesn't try in practice, and pays little attention to his coach. I'm afraid, however, that if we tell him that he can't take lessons or clinics, he'll quit. What should we do? See p. 111   _____   _____

List your toughest issues.

Mother/Father

1.

2.

3.

4.

5.

Player

1.

2.

3.

4.

5.

Coach

1.

2.

3.

4.

5.

1. *My child doesn't want me to watch his matches. Must I comply?*

Invariably when a youngster doesn't want his parents to watch, it's because their presence is adding pressure. And invariably these are parents who have been upset or critical over how the child has played. They've shown negative behavior on the sidelines and in one way or another have created stress for the player.

If you, the parent, want to be at a match, it's difficult to try to hide. If your child absolutely cannot play when you're present and you have to leave courtside, you could take a book, find yourself a quiet corner, and ignore the court. Don't sneak back to the court, trying to find out how the first set went.

A parent in this situation has to realize that the child who demands the parent leave is a child who's felt judged. Indeed, the child still feels that judgment. If the child is cheating and showing unsportsmanlike behavior, you *should* be at courtside—whether your child likes it or not. If your child simply feels that you're watching in order to evaluate his game—that you're concerned about the quality of play—then he won't want you to watch.

Work to correct the way the child is perceiving you. Try not to be critical of the way he plays; be a cheerleader instead. Parents who are cheerleaders are welcome at matches; that's true at all levels of tournament play. When other parents don't want you there, it's because you've become a problem. You've gotten out of hand, stepped across the line. In that rare instance when the player is cheating or showing other unsportsmanlike behavior, the parent should stay and check that behavior.

A supportive parent will prep the child before the match with remarks like these: "I hope you do well. I'm just going to be there, with a newspaper to read." This will indicate that there's no particular concern about the outcome either way, though the parent may be dying inside. The most important thing for parents to remember is not to be threatening.

When the going gets tough—and it will, for everyone—good parents are there with unconditional support, understanding, and love.

2. My daughter shows great promise, but we don't have the money to pay for the kinds of lessons and the travel necessary, as far as we're concerned, for her to reach her full potential. Our only alternative would be to take a second mortgage on our home. Would you advise us to do that?

Several families whose sons and daughters are currently playing junior tennis in fact have done just this. The problem becomes one of guilt. The youngster knows the family is making enormous sacrifices. The youngster also realizes that if she doesn't do well in the next tournament, she isn't doing her fair share. And that belief adds an enormous amount of pressure.

It's not a good idea to make that kind of sacrifice. Parents have to realize that the chance of their daughter's ever playing on the professional tour, and making a lot of money as a result, is next to zero. The more logical goal should be to play college tennis on scholarship and earn an education. But even there, parents are probably better off mortgaging the home for college tuition at a later date than to pay for coaching and junior tournament travel today. A one-year commitment may be a different story. A year's tuition at a tennis academy, for instance, if the parent is confident the experience can substantially change the child's level of play. But the parent has to understand that that is a one-shot attempt, with no conditions placed on the child. The cost has to be underplayed.

3. My son swears and throws his racket during matches and even—on occasion—during practice. What would you suggest we do?

Parents have to be active in situations like this. They have to show and tell the child that sportsmanship and ethical behavior is more important than anything else that happens on the court. The consequences for unsportsmanlike conduct have to be spelled out. If need be, the parent should default the child during a match or prohibit him from playing in the next tournament.

Defaulting should *not* become punishment for poor or lackadaisical playing, however. A parent has to guard against becoming so defensive about the child that she protects him from a bad loss by not letting the match finish. Swearing, racket throwing, abusive language toward the opponent—these are offenses that call for action. The parent should describe the consequences for such outbursts and, when they occur, interrupt the match by walking on to the court and ending the match. Such parental action shouldn't come as a surprise; your child should know exactly what you're thinking. Typically a parent may have to resort to this once, perhaps twice, in a junior's career. The key is explaining to the child that good sportsmanship is *important*—more important than winning.

4. Our daughter's been playing tennis for nearly five years and has not been doing as well as she'd hoped she'd be able to do. She's just told us she'd like to quit. Should we let her?

The parent has to realize that when a child wants to stop competing, either there are other aspects of her life that are taking on importance or the game has become too threatening, and too much of the child's self-esteem is on the line. Before any decision is reached, the parent ought to explore why the child wants to stop playing.

Certainly with most youngsters, taking a break is not a poor first step. During the time off, the parents need to structure how the child gets back into the game. Making the game fun again is a priority. Seeing tennis as casual and enjoyable rather than stressful can be accomplished by rallying together. Ask your child to hit, to give you a little workout. Start innocently. Get the child's peers involved;

make tennis a social activity for the child, not simply a competitive one.

Starting your son or daughter with a group of peers and developing the game with these boys or girls he or she really likes, and learning the game together, is the most effective way to teach the game. An unfortunate syndrome is sending the child off alone to take lessons with a pro as her only involvement with the game. There's no excitement, no connection with peers. As children get older, peers are everything. The best players came up through the age groups in packs, never by themselves.

5. *Our son likes his pro very much, but both my husband and I feel he's a poor coach. What should we do?*

Many children get emotionally attached to their coaches, while parents become critical. Parents may see that the coach mistreats their son or models inappropriate behavior. He or she pushes certain techniques, or overemphasizes winning, or doesn't pay enough one-to-one attention.

Parents have to be keenly aware of the effect a coach is having on the son's self-esteem. Is the coach communicating a sense of fun and enjoyment? Is he giving the son a fair chance? Does he have the necessary skills? Is he a student of the game? Is he lazy? disciplined? well organized? disorganized?

If he lacks the necessary qualities, then the parent has to introduce his replacement carefully—and gradually. If the son is having trouble with the serve, for example, the parent can suggest another pro—perhaps in a neighboring town —with special expertise. By building a bridge to another professional, the son can see that there are others who can help, and can help more than the original coach. If the parent simply yanks the child away from the coach, saying, "You have to go to *this* person," often the child will resent the parent's involvement. The loyalty a child feels toward his teacher is complex; any weaning must be done slowly and carefully.

6. *Our daughter has decided she wants to go to a tennis academy away from home. She's only 14. Should we allow her to go? How can we tell if her personality is right for this step?*

It takes a special set of circumstances to recommend enrollment at a tennis academy. In the best of all worlds, the parents—or one parent—will live in the same community where the academy is located. The research accumulated on academy life to date indicates that children living at home and attending academies succeed more often than those isolated from their families.

Academy life is very stressful for those who have left familiar environs and friends. Many burn out, and others are just not helped. The kind of child who succeeds is typically between ages 14 and 17, is highly motivated, is independent and self-directed, and has lofty but realistic goals. Such a child is driven to become an outstanding player and is capable of hard work and discipline. He or she can say no and is often assertive. Youngsters who are passive don't fare nearly as well. The successful child gets along with peers but isn't overly concerned with their liking him or her and isn't overly sensitive. He or she isn't prone to moodiness or depression, and the parents are supportive but not pushy. In other words, the child who succeeds isn't at an academy for the parents but for herself.

The successful academy student doesn't learn her tennis at the academy either. Most academies are too large to teach the fundamentals. It's the kids who already have the basics who will do well and perhaps thrive in that environment. If your youngster fits that pattern, an academy might make sense.

If the racket could talk, the words would certainly be "dazed, confused, out of sync."

7. *How do we know if the stress levels are too high for our daughter? She's very sensitive and keeps everything inside. What are the signals?*

Everyone has stress barometers, and parents have to help their children tune into them. Poor sleeping habits may be one signal. Irritability or grouchiness may be another. Withdrawal, refusal to converse, poor grades in school—all can indicate too much stress. On the tennis court, nervous play can show stress; so can depression and self-criticism. Parents need to help their children recognize these signals and talk about them.

8. *My son treats me badly when he's not playing well, particularly after he loses. In fact, he treats everyone badly after a loss! Should we accept this as a difficult time and allow it to occur? What can we do?*

First, sit with the child after a tournament has ended and explain that there is no excuse for treating people terribly. Explain that you appreciate how upset he is when he loses but that is no excuse for treating others in an unacceptable way. Suggest that instead, he take 30 minutes after a match to go off by himself—to scream, yell, throw the racket, cry, whatever he wants. But when the child returns, he can't act like a jerk. Quiet, yes—but not like a striking rattlesnake, biting at any remark.

If the son crosses the line, there have to be clear consequences—perhaps taking away tennis, perhaps other privileges. But clearly this is behavior a parent should influence and control. A lot of mistakes are made here by parents who sympathize with the stress and allow children to rage out of control. Parents have to assert themselves and demand their children respect them and others in the family.

9. *Our daughter is not mentally tough, and there are no pros in our area who teach mental toughness training. What would you recommend?*

More and more pros are beginning to get an appreciation of how to train in this area, but it's still not widespread. A number of books and videotapes are available. Because mental toughness focuses on emotional skills, the parent can be very helpful. The more the parent knows, the more help may be given. Seasonal camps with mental toughness classes or monthly sessions with a coach who's had special training can also be helpful. The book, *Mental Toughness Training For Sports*, and the videotape, ''Mental Toughness in Tennis,'' are worth examining if the parent can't get to a pro who teaches this attitude.

10. *Our son is very talented and does well in a number of sports. He's 13 years old and doesn't want to specialize. He likes to play soccer, basketball, and tennis and runs track too. Should we let him play all the sports, or should we get him to focus on one so he will achieve enough skill to be successful?*

The more research is done on athletic success, the more evidence is developed that youngsters who do really well are ones who have played a variety of sports. There's a cross-fertilization from one sport to another, and it helps to keep the child from burning out, from becoming bored or one-dimensional.

Until age 12 to 14, the child should be playing various sports, and the parents should offer encouragement toward that end. The child can gradually focus more and more on tennis, perhaps playing on a year-round basis, but not exclusively.

11. *Our daughter is terribly afraid to play tournaments. She loves to take lessons and loves to hit, but as soon as we suggest a tournament, she freezes. Should we force her to play a few so that she can overcome this, or should we let it go?*

The age of the youngster is a determining factor here. Most people are terrified of playing tournaments, particularly if they're older and have never played one. They're afraid of looking stupid! They hear about USTA tournaments but are intimidated by whom they imagine is entered.

A good place to start is a club round-robin or a small local event—something with an element of competition but populated by friends of the child, familiar faces. You don't jump into USTA tournaments if you have a lot of fear of tournaments. Ease your child into competition and try to ensure some sucess. Take the pressure off and emphasize the enjoyment. If she doesn't do well at first, back off and try again later. Don't even call the competition a tournament. Describe it instead as a round-robin game.

Youngsters should be exposed to competition early—not a tournament but match play. Let it become part of their early development. Someone who has missed this step will never feel comfortable playing tournaments.

12. *Our daughter wants to play every tournament that comes up. Should we let her?*

Parents have to try to determine how stressful tournaments are for the child. Does she get nervous? hyper? Does she show a lot of irritability? sleeplessness? All are indications of competitive trait anxiety syndrome; in other words, the tournament experience is stressful. But she shouldn't be playing many tournaments in a row even if she's doing well. A tournament, then a week off, then another tournament, then another week off. Even if the child is eager, the parent should be concerned about burnout. Better eager than quitter, overwhelmed by it all.

Herb and Aaron Krickstein, father and son—always a delicate balance in tennis.

Structure a summer schedule that helps the child deal with stress. Some kids can play as many as three tournaments in a row before taking a break, but there are not many who can play four, even if they're low-stress personalities. Tournaments are very stressful—and for some kids in the extreme, so make scheduling decisions accordingly.

13. *Our daughter can't stand to talk about her tennis with us. Every time we bring it up, she gets defensive. What can we do?*

This happens often. Indeed, one of our juniors' biggest complaints is that their parents only want to talk tennis. This generally means the parents have become too involved. Tennis discussions have to be balanced by discussions about school, family, and other topics. Tennis is going to have to be avoided.

Following your child's progress and checking with the pro to see how she's faring is fine. But if she doesn't want to talk about the game, then she's feeling your pressure, and you have to back off. Find other topics to talk about; deemphasize tennis—that's what she's saying.

14. Our son is constantly injured. Every time he gets going, he's injured again. It's hard on him emotionally. What can we do?

Recurring injuries can become stressful and are themselves often the product of stress. Such a pattern shouldn't go unexamined by the parent. The child may be pushing too hard, overtaxing a physically immature body. Or the boy's coach may be improperly preparing him for play, either through lack of conditioning or poor technique. A parent ought to be aware of what the child is eating, how much sleep he's getting, how many colds or flus he's getting. If the pattern is tied to competition, restructure the youngster's involvement with the game. Normally there's an answer. In one case, a player suffered from food allergies. In another, it was poor diet. For others, it is excessive stress.

Highly motivated children may have to be led through whatever changes are necessary to prevent injuries. Otherwise they'll return to competition too soon and build further frustration.

15. Our daughter has unrealistic goals. Should we let her pursue them or force her to lower her expectations?

Never take away someone's long-term dream. The parents should simply provide realism for what it would take to reach those goals. What are the necessary steps? How does she know she's on track? What are the benchmarks along the way? These are the ways parents can assist. The parents can also structure the coach's feedback to help her understand she's meeting the criteria to achieve those goals. You give her the chance to change her own goals if she realizes the goal to get a four-year scholarship to Stanford, for example, is not possible. Maybe she'll try to go to a school that has a top-ten ranking or go to a good junior college.

Parental intensity at Kalamazoo. High positive energy is as important for parents as it is for players.

16. *Our son has no discipline in his training. He wants to be good but is inconsistent and irresponsible about arranging for court time, scheduling lessons, and finding practice partners. What should we do?*

Generally when parents try to put discipline into the tennis, the game breaks down. The discipline has to come from the coach. If the parents assume that role, the result—more often than not—is the child's rebellion.

The parent's responsibility is to motivate the coach to take greater interest. That may take money. The parent is asking the coach, in effect, to spend more time thinking about the boy. But the schedule making, goal setting, and charting are all tasks important to any competitive junior success.

Discipline in areas other than tennis can—and should—be taught by the parents. Homework and household chores are responsibilities that, if attended to, will carry over to tennis. But the parent shouldn't try to teach discipline in all areas of life by forcing it upon the child in tennis. And often that's just what parents will do: condone sloppiness off court while demanding a strict adherence to the rules on court.

17. *Our daughter is doing poorly in school. Should we take away tennis as a punishment?*

Tennis ought not to be a tool to promote good grades. If tennis is too dominant and a child is spending too much time on the court (and is too tired to study), a better balance is needed. But simply to threaten to take away tennis if grades don't improve is unfair to the youngster. Tennis is a life experience in much the same way education is. Whatever self-esteem may be gained by succeeding in tennis could be lost through such punishment. Sport can be a means to build confidence for youngsters, and success can spread from one field to another.

Rather than take away tennis, a parent ought to encourage the child to work harder. And if exhaustion is a factor, the child can cut back rather than give up the game.

18. *Is it right for our family to give up vacations and other personal time for our son's tennis? We find ourselves constantly changing our plans to coincide with his tournament schedule. Is that appropriate?*

A lot of parents feel they're giving up a tremendous amount to make the child's tennis experience possible. But the parents have to recognize that their sacrifice is for the experience—not because a return is expected on the investment. Junior competition is an education, and making that education accessible is part of the parental role. The sacrifice isn't to be held over the child's head or used to inflict guilt. If the commitment of time, money, and energy can't be made in that context, then it shouldn't be made. If it has to be thrown into the child's face—"We're doing it for you. We're making these sacrifices. The least you can do is try hard and do well"—it backfires. Yes; let the child be aware of the sacrifice if there's been one. No; don't turn that into a guilt trip.

19. *I see so many young children who've become tennis brats. How does that happen? How can I prevent it happening to my own kids?*

A pitfall for parents can be the knowledge their children are under stress. If the child is winning, parents will overlook some brattiness and irritability just prior to tournaments, when the pressure is the greatest. This constitutes a kind of overinvolvement—ignoring the development of asocial habits because the child

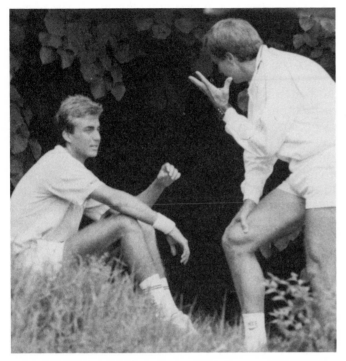

Jim Loehr discusses a hard loss with Hector Navaras at Kalamazoo.

is succeeding. What kind of habits? Insisting that household chores can go undone "because I'm too tired from playing" or demanding transportation ("Pick me up. Take me there"), or treating peers and adults disrespectfully.

The prima donna syndrome—where the person's ego becomes overinflated because of the way he's treated for his tennis accomplishments—is the cause. This message is often communicated covertly; parents don't recognize it consciously. When they do wake up and realize they've got a monster on their hands —spoiled, accustomed to getting his way, refusing to accept a "no" answer to anything—it's tough to realize that the syndrome began with the parent's exaggerated view of the importance of winning for the child.

Trained parents will avoid this syndrome by forcing the child to assume responsibility for his competitive tennis—making his own arrangements, not getting overemotional about either wins or losses. They also should not reward victory or punish defeat. High positive energy on the part of both the parent and the player will eliminate the development of the prima donna.

20. *My son always wants to play sets. When I win—and I'm the better player—he goes crazy. Should I purposely lose to give him confidence?*

Children often want to be competitive, and play competitively, with their parents. This isn't a particularly good situation. Perhaps the parent can play points without keeping score or invent games that don't mean as much as sets, but for most kids, playing parents is tough and develops animosity.

Parents shouldn't be competitive with their children. It's not easy to let a son or daughter win; rather, it's a false sense of confidence that's communicated. If the purpose is to develop confidence, then it's important for the parent to let the child know he's being permitted to win because you, the parent, think that's important. But ultimately other routines—not sets—will serve that purpose better.

21. *I am a teaching pro who teaches her own children. Can that work? The expense of hiring someone else is too great, and there's no one else nearby anyway.*

There are lots of teaching pros and coaches who end up, inevitably, having to work with their own children. This is risky, particularly as the youngsters get better and better. In the beginning stages, this relationship is OK. But most coaches are more critical with—and harder on—their own children, demanding more, than on anyone else. A teaching pro's children will get more pressure from the parent in class and will likely become more sensitive to stress. The parent is making the child's task more difficult when that happens.

In the beginning, though, the arrangement is workable. As the player learns more skills, the chance for conflict increases. As the youngster grows older, the parent-coach ought to shift the responsibility to someone else. Some have had great success in this role, it's true: Gloria and Jimmy Connors, Jim and Chris Evert, Peter and Steffi Graf. But they're in the minority. You have to be a special parent with a special child.

22. *My daughter's 11 years old, and all she wants to do is play tennis. She'd play 10 hours a day if I let her. Is it bad to let her play as much as she likes?*

Yes. The child should always leave the court wanting to play more. Early on, a child can get hooked on tennis, always wanting more. Limiting time on the court, and thereby keeping the youngster eager, reinforces the sense that tennis is an opportunity, something to look forward to.

If you allow a youngster to play all she wants, that eagerness will change. For a while, the interest level will remain high; then boredom will set in. The play will get sloppy; the skills won't develop as quickly; poor habits will set in because the child is tired. The gym-rat syndrome (hanging out all day at the tennis club) is also to be avoided. One day a week at the club won't hurt. But to live at the club for an entire summer, for instance, isn't doing the child a lot of good. The specialness of playing has to be sustained.

23. *Are there any personality patterns that seem to be at a higher risk of burnout than others?*

Yes. The profile of children who tend to have problems with burnout is one of a highly motivated, strongly driven boy or girl who's a perfectionist. These children are critical of themselves, demanding a great deal, and often overachieving. They're going beyond what most people assume they can achieve. They won't say no.

These youngsters are influenced by powerful "oughts" and "shoulds"—what they *could* be doing, what they *ought* to be doing. Their parents have often placed high value on achievement and "doing things right" and have shared with the children perfectionist and outwardly critical traits. Youngsters prone to burnout have strong needs to be liked by both peers and parents, are eager to please, and are sensitive to criticism, even constructive criticism. That seems to go right to their core.

These youngsters are usually lacking in assertive and interpersonal skills. They have difficulty saying no and will do almost anything a coach asks. They don't have sufficient self-direction, self-autonomy, and independence to risk going against the coach and the crowd. They're models of aggressiveness and hard work, rarely discipline problems, trying to fulfill some deep-seated self-esteem needs.

Thomas Muster shows confidence, control, aggressiveness, and poise. Players who are mentally tough look *mentally tough.*

24. *Is there anything I can do constructively while I watch the lessons and matches? Can I take notes or video, for example?*

Whatever the parent does do, it must meet the approval of both the child and the child's coach. It's risky to get involved in any activity that relates, even remotely, to coaching. Talk to the coach and the youngster about what *they* want. If you're the kind of person who can get involved—you understand tennis and you'd like objectively to chart matches—turning the charts over to the coach (letting the coach and the child interpret exactly what your charts indicate) is fine. As long as the child realizes you are doing nothing more than collecting information, that can be a useful task.

If, however, you intrude too far, your youngster will resent you. He won't want you sitting there, evaluating him every minute on every point. He'll get defensive about your making notes every time he makes a mistake—and that will create additional pressure.

Collecting information unobtrusively is an appropriate role. The same holds true for videotaping: as a tool for the coach, fine; as a tool for the parent, a bad idea. Most parents who make a video of a match want to review it for hours and point out the player's strengths and weaknesses. That's the coach's role.

The bottom line is to discover what your child thinks. If the feedback is positive, do it. If not, avoid note taking and cameras.

A player concentrates between points by looking at her strings, demonstrating calmness in the face of adversity.

25. *When should my son travel with a coach? Is it okay that I fill that role if a coach cannot travel?*

As the child becomes more proficient in tennis, he ought to be able to communicate exactly what *he* wants. Having your son periodically travel with a coach is a good experience. It begins to give him increased autonomy, self-direction, and self-sufficiency.

Once a player has begun traveling with a coach, it's not a bad idea for a parent to assume that role on a temporary or acting basis. A parent ought to feel comfortable accompanying his child to a tournament. The parent should not, however, attempt to strategize or coach. Have the child consult with the coach before leaving, and develop a game plan. The parent should be cognizant of that plan, but shouldn't attempt to implement it. Leave that responsibility to the child himself.

26. *How much school should I allow my son or daughter to miss? There always seems to be a tournament that conflicts with academic time. Should tennis be elevated to the same level of importance as school?*

This is a difficult question. Many youngsters at the top junior levels drop out of high school, taking correspondence courses. Others are unfairly penalized because they're missing so much schoolwork, and the pressures of school and tennis combined become too much. For a lot of junior players, one of the primary stresses is school because they don't have enough time or energy to do their work. They're tired when they get home from a tournament (or practice).

Striking a balance here is the parent's responsibility. The parent has to decide which tournaments are important and has to meet with the teachers and explain to them that the youngster isn't simply going away for a holiday but in fact is participating in an experience important to her development. The parent has to be familiar with the school assignments and has to indicate on a schedule—perhaps a calendar that also shows the tournament dates—what work is due when. The parent has to find out from the child's teachers how much time can legitimately be missed and coordinate that with the school.

27. *Should I do all the dirty work? Fetch drinks, towels, regrip rackets, prepare meals, do the laundry, arrange for transportation—who should do all the little things like this? Is that part of the parental role?*

This is part of the tennis training experience. The parent is teaching the child self-sufficiency, discipline, responsibility, and self-directedness. That is the value of tennis. The goal of independence should include all of the above, and reaching that will take time. The child has to learn to be comfortable on his or her own. That requires discipline.

Parents fall into the trap of taking on the dirty work so the child only has to worry about the match. This is a mistake; it fosters dependency. In early tournaments, yes, the parent should perform those chores. But by the time the child is playing in 16- and-under events or even 14-and-under tournaments, the youngster should be exclusively responsible. No one else, even the coach, should be involved in this aspect of their tennis.

28. *Should I set up matches—call people for my daughter—until she learns to do it herself?*

If she won't set up matches, won't call ahead, discussions with both her and her coach are in order. She may simply not want to play. Or she may lack the discipline to think through the process of organizing practice.

Reminders—schedules around the house—should become part of the agreement, or contract, if you will, that's made with the child. If the parent agrees to pay for the lessons, the child agrees to set up the practice schedule. Emphasize that the *coach* feels practice matches should be played on a weekly basis. Set a certain day of the week on which practice has to be arranged. Put it on a calendar. Ask the coach to spend some extra time each week to review that practice schedule with the child. The more the parent does—as the youngster grows older—the more the child resents the adult's involvement. The parent has to orchestrate scheduling through others.

29. *It's a real sacrifice for us to pay for all the lessons and clinics. Our son isn't trying; he's not giving his best effort. He shows up late, doesn't try in practice, and pays little attention to his coach. I'm afraid, however, that if we tell him that he can't take lessons or clinics, he'll quit. What should we do?*

The activity has to relate to the boy's self-esteem and personal needs. In this case, the child seems only remotely connected to tennis. Threats won't work because he doesn't seem to care.

To reestablish the child's interest, get him involved with peers. That's an important link: kids playing together on a consistent basis. If they're taken out of that arena, they'll miss—and be missed by—their friends. Tennis then becomes valuable socially—for the child's needs for recognition, for approval and success. Perhaps a different coach would provide additional motivation or perhaps setting goals that are meaningful to the child will work.

Once the motivation returns, the behavioral patterns will change. The child has to understand that if the parent is sacrificing to pay the tab, there are things he must do—not win, but to take the sport seriously enough to arrive on time, to plan his schedule so there are no complaints from his coach. Otherwise he won't be allowed to play. He's got to understand that his commitment will be part of the process. Some kids may end up quitting for a while. But if a child's friends are involved, the child will eventually reconnect and agree to do the best he can.

As we've noted, these are by no means all the issues junior tennis players and their families will face. When you confront one we haven't covered, jot down a note to yourself and bring it up at a subsequent team meeting. Use communication to turn a tough issue into a manageable one.

6

CONTINUING EDUCATION:
More Stress, More Toughness, Fewer Breakdowns

It's time for the team to review the concept of mental toughness and how it ought to be showing up both on and off the court.

Remember that the development of mental toughness can often be the difference between winning and losing and between a good tennis experience and a bad one. For the parent, mental toughness can be a key tool in maintaining a supportive emotional environment—one that allows the child to handle match play pressure, that makes for productive practice time, and that permits both parent and child to maintain proper perspective. For the child, mental toughness minimizes the chance that a match will be lost through tanking, temper, or choking, as well as making tennis burnout unlikely. Tanking means to give up; to reduce effort and energy and emotionally withdraw. It's an end result of the low negative energy state. Temper means to allow negative emotions to start taking charge. The player feels angry, frustrated, upset, or disappointed. It comes out of the high negative energy state. Choking, the third typical response to pressure, is the inability to follow-through on winning play, to finish off a victory, and is characterized by nervousness and anxiety. A child's ability to control stress on court will extend to off-court stress as well. Nevertheless, almost any player's game breaks down at some point. We'll show the relationship of mental toughness to breakdowns and how to analyze a breakdown in those terms.

Once a junior tennis player has begun competition, the pressures of the sport are fairly evident. Nevertheless, parents—and coaches who've never competed at a high level—often need to be reminded why tennis demands so much mental toughness.

Consider:

In tennis, you're all alone. There are no time-outs, no substitutes. Play must be continuous.

There is virtually no coaching during a match, no help from the outside during competition. Incredible endurance is required; few other sports demand the energy and concentration over an extended period that tennis does. Matches last two or three hours regularly. Occasionally the young player will have two or even three matches in a single day.

Rivalries can produce intense pressure in junior tennis. Sportsmanship must supersede all other considerations.

Tennis is an individual, not a team, sport. And individual sports produce much greater stress levels than team sports. It's a sport where there's a real physical opponent. In many sports that require the same degree of fine motor skill and coordination, there's no physical opponent one must compete against—gymnastics, for example, or diving.

To earn a point, a youngster must actually do something to an opponent. This element of almost personal combat is a great stress producer for young children. The fact that the player makes the decision as to whether the opponent's balls are in or out of the court is another major stress factor. In few sports, will the youngster be required to make precise calls literally separated by inches, a call that may determine the outcome of the match.

The youngster has nowhere to hide; he or she is in public view constantly. Unlike, say, a cross-country runner, there is no opportunity to get out of the central arena for at least some period of time. In tennis, if you break down and have embarrassing moments, you have to stay out there in a visible arena.

In the scoring system, you're never safe. You can never run out the clock because there is no clock. As a result, you're always just a few points from a complete turnaround. The pressure in tennis is relentless. You never can coast. You can never build up such a lead that you can relax about the whole situation.

Tennis is a sport where subtle changes—surfaces, conditions, and so forth—can make substantial differences in the way the game is played, in a player's timing. Tennis is played on a variety of different surfaces. It's typically played outside but on occasion inside. Conditions of wind, sun, and heat provide challenging obstacles emotionally because they can affect timing so crucially. Tennis

In tennis, no matter how bad it gets on court, there is nowhere to hide. If parents do their job, though, there's no reason to hide.

is a fine-motor-skill sport and as such requires precise emotional balance. Any emotional disruptions typically translate into performance problems.

Tennis requires substantial sums of money and thus draws parents into the picture very powerfully. When parents spend the kind of money they have to to keep their sons and daughters in the game, they tend to get interested in the outcome. Parental problems are often the result.

Tennis is one of the only sports where there are national championships at the early ages of 12 and 14. For a youngster to achieve such recognition necessitates criss-crossing the country a minimum of four times a year and playing an extensive tournament schedule. These tournaments often require as many as five matches before one is the victor. The physical demands on young children—the whole concept of a national champion at these young ages—are exceptional in sport.

In most other sports, provisions have been made for designing equipment and rules to accommodate smaller sizes of kids to help them be more successful: smaller basketballs, lower hoops, smaller fields in soccer and football. In tennis, there has been virtually no provision for this. The youngest competitors play on the same sized courts as adults, using the same balls under the same rules. The way an adult wins a point is the way a child wins a point. A smaller racket is usually the only compromise that's made for children, and that's generally only for the youngest.

The skill level for a child to succeed is so high that the frustration a junior experiences is often a result of his or her physical immaturity. That doesn't make the frustration less real.

So again, respect tennis. There are powerful stresses, which lead to real risks.

Young players need parental help and support getting through the tough times in tennis. It's easy to get lost.

SIXTH TEAM MEETING

At this meeting, we want the team to review some facets of mental toughness. We'll discuss again the Ideal Performance State and how the mentally tough player, striving to achieve that state, ought to look and act on the court. Knowing when a player is performing well emotionally is an important asset for all team members. They can reinforce the good behavior with praise and encouragement and discourage inappropriate actions. We'll also highlight how parents can demonstrate mental toughness and what the other members of the team ought to be looking for from them.

Recognition of what can happen when the pressure gets too great is the fundamental exercise for this meeting. The team members will consider what breaks down and how to see that it *is* breaking down. Once again, one hour should be sufficient.

MEETING OUTLINE

1. Discuss mental toughness as it relates to the player.
2. Discuss mental toughness as it relates to the parent.
3. Using the Pressure Goals form, list the ways the player breaks down under pressure.
4. Using the How I as a Tennis Parent Break Down under Pressure form, list the ways the parent breaks down under pressure.

STEP 1

As we've noted, the mentally tough player is one who has learned to trigger a special emotional state during competition, which we've termed the Ideal Performance State. This state is characterized by feelings of high energy, relaxation, calmness, confidence, and enjoyment—high energy. This state is critical to performance. Although pressure or stress can force the body to do things faster or harder or longer, the accompanying emotional distress can render the skill level of that performance lousy. Sure, a bully can give you legs you never knew you had. But could you hit a drop shot as he came at you?

In the Ideal Performance State (IPS), the emotions are balanced; the player is aroused physiologically but not anxious. It literally makes the player perform at his or her very best.

The word *challenge* best describes this state. Challenge, or the challenge response to pressure, connotes the IPS's two most important elements: high energy and positive emotion. Most players respond to adversity and on-court problems by either tanking or temper—two states we defined at the beginning of this chapter. If you tank or show temper, you're not mentally tough.

Choking is the third typical response to pressure. Yes, no one likes to choke or to be thought of as a choker, but it's far superior to tanking or temper. In fact, it's only one step removed from the challenge response. It means, according to our research, that you're trying, that you care, but that your physiology—your body's chemistry—is dominated by reactions generated by fear. All mentally tough athletes occasionally choke. If they don't—and aren't challenging—then they're tanking or showing temper first.

Can team members watch the junior on the court, and determine whether he or she's showing mental toughness? Yes, to a point. There are certain rituals, certain patterns of play consistent in mentally tough tennis. We'll discuss this in step 3, but for the moment, here's what we'd look for if we were on your team:

- A player who's not afraid to be nervous.
- A player who keeps his or her eyes on the strings, on the ground, or on the ball between points.
- A player who executes rituals between and before points to achieve better focus, relaxation, and intensity. Walking, toweling, shadow stroking—the rituals vary from player to player.
- A player who maintains a winning pace between points, especially when angry, nervous, or fatigued. We recommend 16 to 18 seconds between points.
- A player who takes a deep breath between points to help relax and lower the pulse rate and who breathes out at contact, exhaling in an audible "aaah" when hitting the ball.
- A player who projects high positive intensity.
- A player who, even when nervous, shows calmness and relaxation on the outside.
- A player who, following a mistake, simply turns and walks away, as if to say, "No problem."
- A player who, no matter how bad the situation, looks confident, like a fighter.
- A player who refrains from negative self-talk, who encourages himself or herself.
- A player who carries her racket in the nondominant hand, holding it by the throat with the racket head tilted slightly up, as if to say, "When my racket's up, I'm up."

Now discuss whether your child demonstrates mental toughness on court.

Andre Agassi walks away with confidence and poise. The message: ''Give me another one!''

STEP 2

Realize that the parent who's mentally tough is one who doesn't withdraw emotion and tank when the pressure starts to build and the child starts to play badly. Such parents may get nervous, but they don't get upset. They stay challenged, optimistic, and positive. They perform in their own IPS: relaxed, calm, and confident in their son or daughter. As with the child, outward appearance is most important. Nervousness is natural; the trick is not to show it.

Parents in their IPS are problem solvers: supportive, encouraging sportsmanship, not pushy but tough on cheating and unsportsmanlike conduct. What do we mean by sportsmanship? Consider these rules that a mentally tough parent ought to be imparting to the junior player:

- Always be gracious and humble in winning and losing.
- Always shake hands with your opponent at match's end. Shake firmly and look your opponent straight in the eye. Say, "Thanks."
- Study the USTA's code of conduct carefully and play by it.
- Never humiliate or berate your opponent or your own doubles partner.
- Make the best of every on-court situation, regardless of how obnoxious, unfair, or unsportsmanlike your opponent might be.
- Have enough personal class not to resort to whatever ugly behavior the opponent may engage in.
- Value sportsmanship over virtually anything else.
- Always thank the tournament director for having the event.
- If you enter a tournament, you play it unless you are ill or injured.

After all, this is a big part of why the child is playing: to learn how to be a good sportsman.

Finally, a child's esteem should never be on the line in a tennis match. Win or lose, the child needs to know he or she will be loved. Parental approval must not be a prize to be earned with an ace.

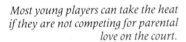

Most young players can take the heat if they are not competing for parental love on the court.

Learning how to deal with pressure on the court is just half the battle. There's pressure off court, too.

STEP 3

How exactly do you, the player, break down under pressure? This is the question we'll get you to try to answer here.

Knowing specifically how you break down under the pressure of big points is the key to correcting it. Once you understand your faulty patterns and competition deficiencies, you can train to correct them. Remember: if you didn't win but should have, something broke down. And for most players, breakdown follows a rather predictable pattern. Rather than responding with all-too-common but rarely productive self-criticism, self-directed anger, or guilt, pursue the question: What broke down? Take each of the following five areas separately, and gradually build a profile of how you typically respond under the pressure of big points.

1. Stroke breakdown. The first question to ask following your match is how your strokes held up on the big points. What strokes, if any, broke down on the big points or in pressure situations? Did your forehand serve or volley let you down when it was critical? Perhaps your approach shot or overhead smash failed as the pressure mounted. If, for instance, your forehand always seems to evaporate on the big points, in all likelihood it's not your head that needs fixing, it's the mechanics of your forehand. The biomechanics of all your strokes must be sound enough that you can play reasonably aggressive tennis—even when you're nervous—without making too many unforced errors. Nervousness is actually a good test for the soundness of any given stroke.

What about your second serve? If you tend to double fault often on the big points, there's a red flag. Of all your strokes, your second serve is the most critical from a pressure perspective. Without a reliable second serve, one that can be hit with aggressiveness and depth under pressure, being tough on the big points is next to impossible. Players rarely connect match toughness with second-serve quality and consistency and as a result rarely practice second serves as a vehicle to improve their mental toughness.

The point is this: players often attribute their poor play on the big points to mental factors, when the real culprit is often a poorly designed stroke; perhaps a slight increase in muscle tightness causes the stroke to collapse. If the same stroke consistently breaks down on the big points, make improving the mechanics of the stroke your number one training strategy for playing the big points better.

2. Strategy breakdown. Many players believe they must do something special and different on big points. As a consequence, they often break from the pattern and style of play that got them to that point. Going for too much too early is a strategy breakdown. Going for the low-percentage winner is particularly tempting on the critical points but generally spells failure. So does suddenly pushing the ball back, hoping your opponent will make an error. Shifting to a conservative, unaggressive style on the big points in order to keep your errors to an absolute minimum will be about as effective as going for too much too soon.

The old dictum—never change a winning game—still holds. Whatever you had been doing to get to the big point, continue doing. As a general rule, you will be most successful if you learn to play offensive, high-percentage tennis on critical points. You become the aggressor and work to get your opponent to make a forced error without making an error yourself.

To do this, you must know your own game well. Your general strategy for big points should be worked out well in advance of your match. And breaking down is when you don't follow it!

3. Emotional breakdown. Players rarely have trouble being positive and energized emotionally on the big points. They know this is a critical time so they generally give 100 percent effort and approach the point positively. So how do you break down emotionally on the big points? The breakdown actually occurs after the point is over, after the critical point has been lost. Becoming a good pressure point player means you do not become overly angry, frustrated, or negative when you lose a big point. Losing an important break point often breaks the player emotionally too. The player fully realizes how important the particular point was and, from that point on, doesn't try as hard and is not as positive. This becomes the deciding factor in the match. So what is an emotional breakdown? It is either the tanking or temper (negative emotions) response.

What about choking? Being nervous on big points is not a breakdown. The fact is that players are likely to be nervous at critical times. The breakdown is determined not by the nervousness but by how the player responds to the nervousness in terms of strokes, strategy, negative emotion, and so forth.

4. Physical breakdown. What you are looking for here are unproductive changes in your physical presence that may occur before, during, or after big points. The following questions reflect such changes: Do you walk faster or take less time on big points? If so, that's a physical breakdown. Do your eyes wander more on the big points, or do you keep your eyes riveted on the strings, ground, or ball between points? Do you stay with your normal pattern of rituals on the big points, such as bouncing the ball, tucking in your shirt, or blowing on your hand before the point starts? How about your breathing? On the crucial points, does the pattern of your breathing change between or during points? Do you project a strong, confident, relaxed image on big points, regardless of how you actually feel? If you lose a big point, do you suddenly look defeated and let your head, racket, and shoulders drag?

Failure to perform consistently in any of these areas will clearly undermine your efforts to play the big points well. Breakdowns here, as in the other areas, follow predictable patterns. Deficiencies in these physical areas have to be dealt with before significant improvement in big-point play can occur.

5. Mental breakdown. As with the physical breakdown, mental breakdown can show itself in several ways. Three stand out: negative thinking, negative self-talk, and negative visualization.

A player who starts thinking negatively begins to reflect on previous bad points. "After losing three set points," she says to herself, "I can never win now." Another might think, "Here I go again, choking the big points away. I'm so bad." When the player starts saying these things out loud, the situation gets worse. It's almost impossible to talk to yourself negatively and play big points well.

Finally, visualization—a powerful tool for playing points well—can have the opposite effect if a player begins to imagine exactly what he or she *doesn't* want to do on the next point. "Don't let me hit the ball into the net," she thinks. The ball goes into the net. "Don't let me double fault." Double fault it is.

Those who play the big points well invariably have learned to picture as clearly and vividly as possible what they want to happen before each point—not what they don't want.

With this in mind, we'd like the team to help the player construct his or her own playing profile. The Pressure Goals form shows the five breakdown areas. In chart 4, we indicate all the possible areas of concern; you can use it for a guide. Team members should help the player focus on which elements apply to him or her. For example, there may be a problem with the second serve and with negative self-talk. Remember, you're asking the player to focus on the *big* points in a match, so a chart prepared by either the coach or the parent will be valuable.

This profile should be an ongoing project. Indeed, it may be enough for the team to identify one or two problems at this meeting and return to the profile at subsequent meetings.

CHART 4
PRESSURE GOALS FORM

Name _____

Date _____

STROKES	PLAYING STRATEGY	EMOTIONALLY	PHYSICALLY	MENTALLY
*1. Serve (1st or 2d)	1. Plays too conservatively Pushes Plays not to lose	1. Tank/low intensity	*1. Physical fitness	1. Negative self-talk
2. Forehand		2. Anger (negative emotions)	**2. Eyes	2. Negative imaging before start of point
3. Backhand		3. Choke (fear, anxiety, nervousness)	3. Rituals	3. Negative thinking
*4. Return of serve	2. Plays too aggressively Overhits 1st or 2d ball winners		4. Winning pace	*4. Visualizes vividly what player wants to have happen on the point before starting the point.
5. Volley Forehand Backhand	*3. Plays high percentage aggressive tennis under pressure	*4. Challenge is the response of the mentally tough competitor. It is *learned*!	5. Breathing	
6. Overhand			6. High positive intensity	*#4 is the response of great competitors.
			7. Mistake management	
*If 2d serve or return of serve break down, raise a red flag. These are the two most important strokes from a pressure perspective. If there is a problem, get to work on them today.	*#3 is your goal. Getting your opponent to make a forced error and keeping your errors to a minimum.	*#4 is the response of great competitors.	8. Confident fighter	
			9. Negative self-talk	
			10. Positive attitude	
			11. "I love the battle"	
			12. Racket up	
			*Without physical fitness, mental toughness is impossible.	
			**See page 121, item 4 of the workbook for explanations.	

© James E. Loehr, 1987

PRESSURE GOALS 125

Name _____

Date _____

Instructions: List under the appropriate column what typically happens under pressure. Then list some possible remedies for these problems.

☐ **Under Pressure—What am I Going to do?**

STROKES	PLAYING STRATEGY	EMOTIONALLY	PHYSICALLY	MENTALLY

© James E. Loehr, 1987

STEP 4

Now, it's the parents' turn. We want the parents to examine how *they* act under pressure, just as the child has. Mental toughness is easy when winning, when things are going well. But how does the parent's attitude and behavior change when problems arise?

Team parents should ask themselves: Do I become more critical? Do I show less support? Am I less sensitive? Do I apply more pressure? Do I become more negative? Am I less patient?

Finally, we want the parents to consider whether their emotional response is to tank, to show anger or temper, to choke, or to demonstrate the challenge response. Remember: the parental response will affect and perhaps complicate the child's task of achieving the Ideal Performance State.

Now it's time to be honest on paper. Each parent should describe how he or she breaks down under pressure, using the How I as a Tennis Parent Break Down under Pressure form. The rest of the team can—and should—help out here.

In the end, mental toughness is not a substitute for well-grounded strokes, all-around athleticism, or top physical condition. But when most other things are equal, the mentally tough player—and the team that practices mental toughness—will succeed.

The connection between eating right and mental toughness is real. Training right includes eating right.

1. _____
_____
_____

How this affects my child's Ideal Performance State (IPS): _____
_____
_____
_____

2. _____
_____
_____

How this affects my child's IPS: _____
_____
_____
_____

3. _____
_____
_____

How this affects my child's IPS: _____
_____
_____

1. _____

_____

_____

How this affects my child's Ideal Performance State (IPS): _____

_____

_____

2. _____

_____

_____

How this affects my child's IPS: _____

_____

_____

3. _____

_____

_____

How this affects my child's IPS: _____

_____

_____

7

RULES FOR PLAY: The USTA Rules and Some Training Guidelines

Knowing the rules of the game and what's expected by the rulemakers is a crucial aspect of competition. In this chapter, we provide a summary of the rules of tennis prepared by the United States Tennis Association (USTA), and the association's standards of conduct. We also present some general training guidelines for the player and coach to consider. That training is their prerogative, and parents shouldn't interfere with the schedule, unless—obviously—it's wreaking havoc on home life and creating a negative emotional environment. We've also listed the addresses of all sections of the USTA. Since the vast majority of junior tennis tournaments are supervised at the section level, any team embarking on a junior competitive schedule will be going to its local section for a calendar of events. Those calendars will be available by writing the appropriate section.

SEVENTH TEAM MEETING

Before the meeting, have each team member review how the junior tennis system works and the USTA's Standards of Conduct.

Using the customary hour, have each team member write down in list form questions that come to mind based on hypothetical or real situations they've encountered. Because there is little other writing associated with this meeting, we suggest you review some of the written reports and forms that proved troublesome in previous meetings. Problems and issues that appeared thorny early on may seem less so by now.

There are 17 sectional associations in the USTA's junior tennis system. These can cover entire regions of the country, such as New England's six states, or just part of one state. Southern and northern California, for example, have their own sections (see p. 136). The sections administer the USTA's regional affairs and host most of the USTA's junior tournaments. Only tournaments sanctioned by the USTA are used for ranking purposes, and rankings are listed annually in four divisions: 18 and under, 16 and under, 14 and under, and 12 and under—for boys and girls separately. There are various requirements for ranking, including a minimum number of tournaments played, head-to-head wins and losses with other ranked players, and a level of commitment.

The USTA has issued a manual for all junior players that is a must to read. It can be obtained by writing to: United States Tennis Association, 1212 Avenue of the Americas, New York, NY, 10036. One of the most important points made in this handbook is that USTA junior rankings do not necessarily describe who is the better player. Among the points the manual makes are these:

1. A ranking is not a measure of a player's skill but a statement about the result of competitive encounters.
2. Rankings aren't based on how far a player gets in tournaments. Who one's opponents are is much more important.
3. Scores are irrelevant. Winning a set but losing the match doesn't help a player to move up, nor does losing a set to a weaker player cause a downward move.
4. Seedings and rankings are not interchangeable. Tournament committees are free to use their own formulas for seedings.
5. Sectional and national rankings aren't identical. A lower-ranked sectional player can have a higher national ranking than a regional peer if the lower-ranked player does better in national events.
6. Rankings don't weigh time of year. On a January–December calendar, an early season win is as important as one in the fall.
7. Players are responsible for getting their records to ranking committees. And hype—press clippings and such—cannot help.

SECTIONAL ASSOCIATIONS OF THE USTA

NORTH ATLANTIC REGION

1. NEW ENGLAND—P.O. Box 223, Needham, MA 02192 617/444-1332
   Comprising the states of Maine, Massachusetts, New Hampshire, Rhode Island, Vermont, and, the state of Connecticut excepting that part which is within 35 miles of New York City Hall (which shall form part of the Eastern section) but including that part of the state of Connecticut which is within the city limits of Stamford.
2. EASTERN—202 Mamaroneck Avenue, White Plains, NY 10601 914/946-3533
   Comprising the state of New York. Of the state of Connecticut, that part which is within 35 miles of New York City Hall, excepting that part which is within the city limits of Stamford. Of the following counties, boroughs, and townships in the state of New Jersey; all of the counties of Passaic, Bergen, Essex, Union, and Hudson; all of Monmouth County except the following townships and boroughs: Manasquan, Sea Girt, Spring Lake Heights, Avon-by-the-Sea, Bradley Beach, Neptune, Neptune City, South Belmar, Belmar, Wall, Howell, Farmingdale, Millstone, Roosevelt, Upper Freehold, Allentown, Briele, Freehold, Freehold Township, Manalapan, and Englishtown; all of Middlesex County except the following townships and boroughs: Cranbury, South Brunswick, Plainsboro, Jamesburg, and Monroe; all of Somerset County except the following townships and boroughs: Rocky Hill, Montgomery, Hillsborough, Branchburg, and Bedminster; all of Morris County except the following townships and boroughs: Chester Township, Chester, Washington, Mount Olive, Netcong, Roxbury, and Mount Arlington. Contains the following district tennis association: Staten Island.

3. MIDDLE STATES—939 Radnor Road, Wayne, PA 19087 215/688-4040
Comprising the states of Pennsylvania, Delaware, the West Virginia counties of Brooke, Hancock, Marshall, and Ohio and the state of New Jersey except that portion thereof allocated to Eastern as above set forth. Contains the following district tennis associations: Delaware, Central Pennsylvania, Lehigh Valley, Philadelphia, New Jersey, Allegheny Mountain.

SOUTHERN REGION

4. MID-ATLANTIC—P.O. Drawer F, Springfield, VA 22151-0180 703/321-9045
Comprising the District of Columbia and the states of Maryland, Virginia (except the city limits of Bristol), and West Virginia, except the following counties therein: Boone, Brooke, Cabell, Calhoun, Hancock, Jackson, Kanawha, Lincoln, Logan, Marshall, Mason, Mingo, Ohio, Pleasants, Putnam, Ritchie, Roane, Wayne, Wirt, and Wood. Contains the following district tennis associations: Washington, D.C., Maryland, West Virginia, Virginia.
5. SOUTHERN—3121 Maple Drive, N.E., #29, Atlanta, GA 30305 404/237-1319
Comprising the states of Alabama, Arkansas, Georgia, Kentucky (except Boone, Campbell, and Kenton Counties), Louisiana, Mississippi, North Carolina, South Carolina, Tennessee; and, of the state of Texas, Bowie County, and the city limits of Bristol, Virginia. Contains the following district tennis associations: Alabama, Arkansas, Georgia, Kentucky, Louisiana, Mississippi, North Carolina, South Carolina, Tennessee.
6. FLORIDA—9620 N.E. 2nd Avenue, Room 209, Miami Shores, FL 33138 305/757-8568
Comprising the state of Florida.
7. CARIBBEAN—P.O. Box 40456, Minillas Sta., Santurce, PR 00940 809/725-6407
Comprising Puerto Rico and the U.S. Virgin Islands of St. Thomas, St. Croix, and St. John. Contains the following district tennis associations: Puerto Rico, Virgin Islands.

CENTRAL REGION

8. WESTERN—2242 Olympic Street, Springfield, OH 45503 513/390-2740
Comprising the states of Illinois (except Rock Island and that part of Illinois within a 30-mile radius of St. Louis City Hall), Indiana, Michigan, Ohio, Wisconsin, excepting the counties of Barron, Bayfield, Buffalo, Burnett, Chippewa, Douglas, Dunn, Eau Claire, Pepin, Pierce, Polk, Rusk, St. Croix, Sawyer, Trempealeau, and Washburn, that portion of Kentucky included in the counties of Boone, Campbell, and Kenton, that portion of West Virginia in the counties of Boone, Cabell, Calhoun, Jackson, Kanawha, Lincoln, Logan, Mason, Mingo, Pleasants, Putnam, Ritchie, Roane, Wayne, Wirt, and Wood. Contains the following district tennis associations: Central Indiana, Chicago, Northern Michigan, Northeastern Michigan, Southeastern Michigan, Western Michigan, Northern Indiana, Middle Illinois, Northern Illinois, Ohio Valley, Northeastern Ohio, Northwestern Ohio, Southern Illinois, Wisconsin.
9. NORTHWESTERN—5525 Cedar Lake Road, St. Louis Park, MN 55416 612/546-0709
Comprising the states of Minnesota, North Dakota, South Dakota; and, of the state of Wisconsin, the counties of Barron, Bayfield, Buffalo, Burnett, Chippewa, Douglas, Dunn, Eau Claire, Pepin, Pierce, Polk, Rusk, St. Croix, Sawyer, Trempealeau, and Washburn.

10. MISSOURI VALLEY—722 Walnut, Suite 1, Kansas City, MO 64106 816/556-0777
Comprising the states of Iowa, Kansas, Missouri, Nebraska, Oklahoma, that part of Illinois known as Rock Island County, and that part of Illinois within a 30-mile radius of St. Louis City Hall. Contains the following district tennis associations: Heart of America, Iowa, Kansas, Nebraska, Oklahoma, St. Louis.

PACIFIC REGION

11. TEXAS—P.O. Box 192, Austin, TX 78767 512/443-1334
Comprising the state of Texas, except El Paso and Bowie Counties.
12. SOUTHWESTERN—3228 E. Indian School Road, Suite 107, Phoenix, AZ 85018 602/955-2546
Comprising the states of Arizona and New Mexico, together with El Paso County, Texas. Contains the following district tennis associations: Southern Arizona, Phoenix, Greater El Paso, Northern New Mexico.
13. INTERMOUNTAIN—1201 S. Parker Rd. #102, Denver, CO 80231 303/695-4117
Comprising the states of Colorado, that part of Idaho south of the 45th parallel of latitude, Montana (except Lincoln County), Nevada (except for the counties of Washoe and Carson City), Utah, Wyoming. Contains the following district tennis associations: Southern Nevada, Colorado, Southern Idaho, Montana, Utah, Central Utah, Northern Utah, Wyoming.
14. PACIFIC NORTHWEST—10175 S.W. Barbur Blvd., #306B, Portland, OR 97219 503/245-3048
Comprising the states of Alaska, Oregon, Washington, (that part of Idaho north of the 45th parallel of latitude, and Lincoln County, Montana), and the province of British Columbia.
15. NORTHERN CALIFORNIA—645 Fifth Street, San Francisco, CA 94107 415/777-5683
Comprising the counties of Alameda, Alpine, Amador, Butte, Calaveras, Colusa, Contra Costa, Del Norte, El Dorado, Fresno, Glenn, Humboldt, Inyo, Kings, Lake, Lassen, Madera, Marin, Mariposa, Mendocino, Merced, Modoc, Mono, Monterey, Napa, Nevada, Placer, Plumas, Sacramento, San Benito, San Francisco, San Joaquin, San Mateo, Santa Clara, Santa Cruz, Shasta, Sierra, Siskiyou, Solano, Sonoma, Stanislaus, Sutter, Tehama, Toulumme, Trinity, Tulare, Yolo, and Yuba in the state of California and the counties of Washoe and Carson City in the state of Nevada.
16. SOUTHERN CALIFORNIA—P.O. Box 240015, Los Angeles, CA 90024 213/208-3838
Comprising the counties of Imperial, Kern, Los Angeles, Orange, Riverside, San Bernardino, San Diego, San Luis Obispo, Santa Barbara, Ventura. Contains the following district association: San Diego.
17. HAWAII PACIFIC—3538 Waialae Avenue, #207, Honolulu, HI 96816 808/735-3008
Comprising the state of Hawaii and the territories of American Samoa and Guam. Contains the following district tennis associations: American Samoa, Guam, Hawaii, Kauai, Maui.

MEETING OUTLINE

1. Read the USTA Standards of Conduct, and the summary of the rules of tennis (reprinted here).
2. Using blank sheets of paper, all members should list the issues they'd like to discuss involving the standards of conduct or tennis rules.
3. Discuss the issues.
4. Review tennis training guidelines (reprinted here).

STEP 1

We reprint in the appendixes at the end of this chapter the USTA's Standards of Conduct and the summary of the rules of tennis. Read them.

STEP 2

Prepare a list of issues or questions that the Standards of Conduct raise in your mind. These can be hypothetical or based upon something you actually saw at a tournament. A player might ask: What should I do if I know I'm getting cheated and there are no linesmen available? A parent's question might be: Am I allowed to say anything to my child during matches? What is considered coaching?

STEP 3

Keeping in mind your review of how the junior tennis system works, discuss ranking procedures with your coach, and make certain he or she feels comfortable with the level the junior is competing at. Have you seen the USTA's junior handbook? If not, perhaps you should write for it.

STEP 4

Review the following general tennis training guidelines. Do yours correspond? Does your coach agree or disagree with these? Parents should make sure they understand the training their child is getting and can be fully supportive:

GENERAL TRAINING GUIDELINES

- Training should always include the stress cycle and the recovery cycle. Recovery is just as important in performance as stress.
- The work stimulus should be administered in gradual increments. Too much running, too many sit ups, too much sprinting too soon leads to breakdown.
- Hard training days should be followed by easy ones, particularly in strength and power training.
- Whenever possible, training should be done in cycles. Early phases of the cycle should focus on building a strong aerobic and endurance base. This may last anywhere from three to five weeks. During this phase of training, virtually no match play, no competitive activity, no fine motor skill practice is conducted. Distance running and cycling, on-court endurance drilling (slow, easy hitting and running for long periods of time), and slow, endurance strength training are generally recommended. In the middle phase of training, very little, if any, aerobic work is done. The training now shifts gradually to strengthening the

anaerobic, speed, and power systems. This can last from one to several months. Competitive play is gradually reintroduced into the training schedule; shorter distances, faster times, quickness, speed of reactions, sprints, and so on become the core of the off-court training. On-court activities in the form of both drill and match play reflect this training emphasis. Fine-motor-skill training is again appropriate during this phase. The final phase is the pretournament or peaking phase. The emphasis here is on duplicating the conditions of match play as precisely as possible. On an average, tennis is played on a ratio of 1 to 2: 10 seconds of playing time followed by 20 seconds of recovery. This is referred to as an alactic anaerobic activity (high-intensity output for short periods of time). During this final phase, all training activities should be tailored to produce brief and explosive, high-intensity output. The final days prior to tournament play should be designed so that stress levels are reduced and the recovery cycle is complete before playing. Being fresh, eager, and fully recovered physically and emotionally is essential for optimal tournament play.

- Adjustments in training cycles will be necessary to allow for individual tournament schedules. Discussions about most important tournaments, when to peak, training restrictions while traveling, and other issues must be held and reflected in the overall cycle.
- Avoid practicing fine-motor skills when you are tired or fatigued.
- Short practice sessions of high intensity are preferable to long sessions with moderate to low intensity, particularly as competition approaches.
- Do not combine long-distance endurance work with fine-motor-skill training, and do not do long-distance training prior to or during competitive events.
- Be careful not to overtrain *before* tournaments. Players often put so much effort and energy into playing practice matches that they arrive overly stressed and generally fatigued.
- Be careful not to overtrain *during* tournaments. Too many players overtrain during tournaments thinking they must hit thousands of balls or they won't play well.
- Players should take at least one full day off from training each week. That means no tennis, no running, no physical or emotional tennis stress. The word is *relaxation*.

Standards of Conduct

All players in and officials and organizers of any tennis tournament, match or exhibition are under a duty to encourage and maintain high standards of proper conduct, fair play and good sportsmanship. The use of banned substances is prohibited and the detection of, and penalties for, any such use shall be in conformity with the policy and regulations of the United States Olympic Committee to the extent applicable as determined by the Board of Directors.

Players are under an obligation to avoid acts which may be considered detrimental to the game of tennis. Such detrimental acts include, but are not limited to, the following:

(i) Entering two or more tournaments, matches or exhibitions scheduled to take place at the same time, in whole or in part, unless each committee (or whoever is in charge) involved understands the situation and concurs in writing with such arrangements as are made;

(ii) Entering a tournament with the intention of withdrawing if the player's entry is accepted in another tournament, unless the tournament committee for the tournament in which the player has entered understands the situation and concurs with such contemplated action;

(iii) Entering a tournament and then failing to appear for a match (whether in the qualifying, main or consolation draw), except for illness, injury or personal emergency;

(iv) Defaulting in a tournament (whether during the course of a match or prior to the commencement of a match and whether in the qualifying, main or consolation draw), except for illness, injury or personal emergency;

(v) After entries have closed, withdrawing from a tournament, except for a bona fide reason;

(vi) After the draw has been made, withdrawing from a tournament, except for illness, injury or personal emergency;

(vii) During the course of a match—to swear at an official, a spectator or an opponent in a voice that can be heard by any person; to use profanity or insulting, abusive or obscene language in any way that may be heard by any person; to use obscene, insulting or abusive gestures; to throw in any manner a racquet or to deliberately throw or hit a ball in the direction of an official or the spectators; to threaten bodily injury to anyone;

(viii) Associating with professional gamblers;

(ix) Betting or acting as a bookmaker on matches;

(x) Accepting money or other consideration for losing a match, or for winning by only a particular margin;

(xi) Being a party to any payment of money or other consideration to another person to induce such person to lose a match, or to win by only a particular margin;

(xii) Reporting or commenting in the press, radio or television for money or other consideration concerning, and during the time of, any tournament, match or exhibition in which the player is or was entered as a competitor.

The tournament committee may, if it so desires, require that any player who withdraws from a tournament after the draw has been made and prior to the commencement of play, because of illness or injury:

(i) obtain a verification of such illness or injury from a doctor (medicine or osteopathy);

(ii) notify the tournament chairman or referee by telephone or telegram of such illness or injury immediately after such player determines that he or she will be unable to play; and

(iii) deliver or mail such a verification to the tournament chairman or referee within four days from the date such player determines that he or she will be unable to play.

If the tournament committee desires to impose such a requirement, a notice of such requirement must be included in the materials furnished to players in connection with their entry into the tournament (e.g., entry blank, tournament brochure or list of rules).

In addition, the tournament committee may, if it so desires, require that any player who defaults after the commencement of play, because of illness or injury, must obtain a verification of such illness or injury from a doctor. If the tournament committee desires to impose such an additional requirement, the tournament committee must, at the tournament's expense, provide the services of a doctor to examine such player (it being understood that the player may elect, at his or her expense, to obtain the services of another doctor, in which case the player must do so without delay), and a notice of such requirement must be included in the materials furnished to players in connection with their entry into the tournament.

The Chairman of any tournament, match or exhibition may withhold all or part of any prize money or expenses payable to any player charged by such Chairman or by the Referee of such event with conduct inconsistent with the above standards, provided a written complaint of such conduct is promptly filed with the Chairman of the Grievance Committee. Any prize money or expenses so withheld shall be withheld until a final determination of the charges in such complaint has been made in accordance with Section 41 of the By-Laws. Immediately after such final determination, the funds withheld, less amount of any fine, shall be promptly paid to the player, and the funds representing the amount of the fines shall be promptly paid to the USTA.

Appendix 7B

Summarized Rules of Tennis

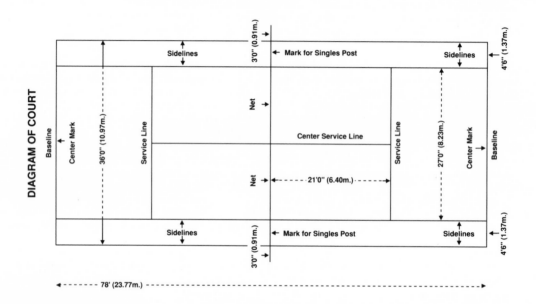

DIAGRAM OF COURT

INTRODUCTION

The official rules of tennis are summarized below for the convenience of all players. In the preparation of this summary, no changes were made in the official rules, which have been established by the International Tennis Federation and are adhered to by the United States Tennis Association. Some technical aspects, however, such as specifications on court size and equipment, balls and rackets, have been deleted here for the sake of brevity. For those who are interested in these specifications, they are covered in their entirety in the complete *Rules of Tennis*, which also includes interpretative Cases and Decisions and USTA Comments.

A familiarity with these rules and traditions is essential for achieving the greatest possible benefit and enjoyment from tennis.

THE SINGLES GAME

Server and Receiver

The players stand on opposite sides of the net; the player who first delivers the ball is called the Server and the other, the Receiver.

Choice of Sides and Service

The choice of sides and the right to be Server or Receiver in the first game is decided by toss. The player winning the toss may choose or require his opponent to choose: (a) the right to be Server or Receiver, in which case the other player shall choose the side; or (b) the side, in which case the other player shall choose the right to be Server or Receiver.

Delivery of Service

The service is delivered in the following manner: immediately before commencing to serve, the Server positions himself with both feet at rest behind the baseline and within the imaginary continuation of the center mark and the sideline of the singles court. He shall not serve until the Receiver is ready.

The Server then throws the ball into the air in any direction and strikes it with his racket before it hits the ground. Delivery is deemed complete at the moment the racket strikes the ball.

Return of Service

The Receiver may stand wherever he pleases on his own side of the net. However, he must allow the ball to hit the ground before returning service. If the Receiver attempts to return the service, he shall be deemed ready.

Service from Alternate Courts

In delivering the service, the Server stands alternately behind the right and left courts, beginning from the right in every game. The ball served shall pass over the net and hit the ground within the service court which is diagonally opposite, or upon any linee bounding such court, before the Receiver returns it.

If the ball is erroneously served from the wrong half of the court, the resulting play stands, but service from the proper court, in accordance with the score, shall be resumed immediately after this discovery.

Faults

The service is a fault if the Server misses the ball in attempting to serve it, if the ball does not land in the proper service court, or if the ball served touches a permanent fixture other than the net, strap or band before it hits the ground.

Throughout the delivery of the service, the Server shall keep both feet behind the baseline and shall not change his position by walking or running. A foot fault is called when the Server steps on the baseline or into the court before his racket meets the ball.

Service After a Fault

After a first fault, the Server serves again from behind the same half of the court from which he served that fault (unless it was a fault because he served from behind the wrong half, in which case he is entitled to deliver one service from behind the proper half).

A Service Let

During the service, a ball that touches the net but lands in the proper court is termed a "let" and counts for nothing. That one service is replayed. There is no limit to the number of let balls that may be made on the service; the Server continues serving into the same court until a good service is delivered or two faults are made.

Receiver Becomes Server

At the end of the first game, the Receiver becomes Server and the Server, Receiver; and so on alternately in all the subsequent games of a match. The players change sides at the end of the first, third and every subsequent alternate game.

If a player serves out of turn, the player who ought to have served shall serve as soon as the mistake is discovered. All points scored before such discovery shall stand. If a game has been completed before such discovery, the order of service remains as altered.

Server Wins Point

The Server wins the point if the ball served, not being a let, touches the Receiver or anything which he wears or carries before it hits the ground or if the Receiver otherwise loses the point as described below.

Receiver Wins Point

The Receiver wins the point if the Server serves two consecutive faults or otherwise loses the point as described below.

Ball Falling on Line—Good

A ball falling on a line is regarded as falling in the court bounded by that line.

Player Loses Point

A player loses the point if:
  (a) he fails to return the ball in play directly over or past the end of the net before it has hit the ground twice consecutively; or
  (b) he returns the ball in play so that it hits the ground, a permanent fixture (other than the net, posts or singles sticks, cord or metal cable, strap or band), or other object outside any of the lines which bound his opponent's court; or
  (c) he deliberately carries or catches the ball in play or his racket or deliberately touches it with his racket more than once; or
  (d) he or his racket touches the net, post or the ground within his opponent's court at any time while the ball is in play; or
  (e) he volleys the ball before it has passed the net; or
  (f) he volleys the ball and fails to make a good return even when standing outside the court; or
  (g) he throws his racket at and hits the ball; or
  (h) he deliberately and materially changes the shape of his racket during the playing of the point; or
  (i) he deliberately commits any act which hinders his opponent in making a stroke; or
  (j) the ball in play touches him or anything that he wears or carries other than the racket in his hand.

A Good Return

It is a good return if:
  (a) the ball touches and passes over the net, posts, cord or metal cable, strap or band and hits the ground within the court; or
  (b) the ball touches any other permanent fixture after it has hit the ground within the proper court; or
  (c) the ball hits the ground within the proper court and rebounds back over the net and the player whose turn it is to strike reaches over the net and plays the ball, provided that neither he nor any part of his clothes or racket touches the net, and that the stroke is otherwise good; or
  (d) the ball is returned from outside the post, provided that it hits the ground within the proper court; or
  (e) a player's racket passes over the net after he has properly returned the ball; or
  (f) a player succeeds in returning the ball which has struck another ball lying in the court.

A Let

In all cases where a let (other than a service let) has to be called under the rules or to provide for an interruption of play, the point shall be replayed.

If a player is hindered in making a stroke by anything not within his control, except a permanent fixture or deliberate interference by his opponent, a let shall be called.

Coaching

A player may not receive coaching during the playing of any match other than one that is part of a team competition.

THE DOUBLES GAME

The above Rules apply to the Doubles Game except as below.

Delivery of Service

The Server positions himself with both feet at rest behind the baseline and within the imaginary continuation of the center mark and the sideline of the doubles court.

Order of Service

At the beginning of each set, the pair serving the first game decides which partner shall do so and the opposing pair decides similarly for the second game. The partner of the player who served in the first game serves in the third; the partner of the player who served in the second game serves in the fourth, and so on in the same order in all subsequent games of a set.

Order of Receiving

The pair receiving the service in the first game of each set decides which partner shall receive in the right-hand court, and the opposing pair decides similarly in the second game of each set. Partners receive the service alternately throughout each game. The order of receiving the service shall not be altered during the set but may be changed at the beginning of a new set.

Service Out of Turn

If a partner serves out of his turn, the partner who ought to have served shall serve as soon as the mistake is discovered, but all points scored and any faults served before such discovery shall stand. If a game has been completed before such discovery, the order of service remains as altered.

Receiving Out of Turn

If during a game the order of receiving the service is changed by the Receivers, it remains as altered until the end of the game, but the partners shall resume their original order of receiving in the next game of that set in which they are the Receivers.

Served Ball Touching Player

The service is a fault if the ball touches the Server's partner or anything which he wears or carries. The Server wins the point if the ball served (not being a let) touches the partner of the Receiver, or anything he wears or carries, before it hits the ground.

Ball Struck Alternately

The ball shall be struck by one or the other player of the opposing pairs in the course of making a serve or a return. If both of them hit the ball, either simultaneously or consecutively, their opponents win the point.

SCORING

A Game

If a player wins his first point, the score is called 15 for that player; on winning his second point, his score is called 30, on winning his third point, his score is called 40; and the fourth point won by a player is scored a Game for that player except as follows:

If both players have won three points, the score is called Deuce; the next point won by a player is scored Advantage for that player. If the same player wins the next point, he wins the Game. If the other player wins the next point, the score is again called Deuce; and so on, until a player wins the two points immediately following the score at Deuce, when the Game is scored for that player.

A Set

A player (or players) who first wins six games wins a Set, except that he must win by a margin of two games over his opponent. Where necessary, a Set is extended until this margin is achieved (unless a tie-break system of scoring has been announced in advance of the match).

The players change sides at the end of the first, third, and every subsequent alternate game of each set and at the end of each set unless the total number of games in such set is even, in which case the change is not made until the end of the first game of the next set.

The maximum number of sets in a match is five for men and three for women.

The Tie-Break Game

If announced in advance of the match, a Tie-break Game operates when the score reaches six games all in any set.

In singles, a player who first wins seven points wins the game and the set provided he leads by a margin of two points. If the score reaches six points all the game is extended until this margin has been achieved. Numerical scoring is used throughout the Tie-break Game. The player whose turn it is to serve is the Server for the first point; his opponent is the Server for the second and third points; and, thereafter, each player serves alternately for two consecutive points until the winner of the game and set has been decided.

In doubles, the player whose turn it is to serve is the Server for the first point. Thereafter, each player serves in rotation for two points, in the same order as determined previously in that set, until the winners of the game and set have been decided.

From the first point, each service is delivered alternately from the right and left courts, beginning from the right court. The first Server serves the first point from the right court; the second Server serves the second and third points from the left and right courts, respectively; the next Server serves the fourth and fifth points from the left and right courts, respectively; and so on.

Players change ends after every six points and at the conclusion of the Tie-break Game. The player (or doubles pair) who served first in the Tie-break Game shall receive service in the first game of the following set.

ROUTINE MAINTENANCE

All the groundwork has been completed for a successful team. Now comes the routine maintenance. In order to keep the lines of communication open in all directions, team members have to continue to schedule regular meetings. We'd suggest once a month, although one every two months or three may be suitable if your child is playing a reduced tournament schedule.

Why keep the meetings going? Because problems evolving from new situations will constantly arise. Every tournament is different, every year of play more sophisticated, more complex, more stressful. Is the coach adapting? Is the child? Is the parent?

You may want to return, on an annual basis, to some of the early forms, to see whether your attitudes have changed. You may also want to review from time to time chapters 5 and 6, with their situational analysis and recommendation on how to avoid breakdowns.

Finally, we've included some additional mental toughness feedback forms. Wait six months or so and then have the team try one of these new forms as the focus for a regular meeting. Above all, maintain composure and a relaxed focus about competition. That's the way to succeed.

Fractions of inches can separate winners from losers. From a parental perspective, however, the child can never be a loser. The message must be "win or lose, I love you just the same"—and it must be meant.

TESTING FOR TOUGHNESS

Included here are a variety of self-administered questionnaires provided to help players evaluate their emotional control and mental toughness.

Begin with the Psychological Performance Inventory for Sports. In this inventory, the player first reads the list describing various emotional responses to competition. Each sentence—there are 42 in all—describes an emotional state. The player is asked to consider the extent to which the description is applicable to him or her and mark that answer in the answer section.

Parent and player together can then graph the responses using the summary portion of the form. The graphing is relatively simple. Every answer the player gives receives a numerical score. On the answer sheet, some of the questions have lines under their identifying number; others don't. For the questions without underlining, the answers are valued from 1 (Almost Always) to 5 (Almost Never). For questions with underlining, the scoring is reversed. Almost Always is worth 5; Almost Never is worth 1. If a player reads "I see myself more of a loser than a winner as a competitor," and answers "Often," that answer is worth 4 points. If the same player on item 11—"I mentally practice my physical skills"—responds "Seldom," that, too, is worth 4 points.

The scores are added on the summary sheet and then transferred to the graph, which allows parent, player, and coach to assess the relative strengths and weaknesses of the player's mental game.

Any score below 20 in any of the seven broad categories—self-confidence; negative energy control; attention control; visual and imagery control; motivational level; positive energy control; and attitude control—ought to raise a red flag. There's a deficiency there, and it's something the player should address. The parent and the coach should understand it's an area needing special attention. A score between 20 and 25 indicates competence in the area. Anything over 25 suggests great strength, an enhancing skill.

A related feedback form, which has also proved invaluable to academy students, is the Post Competition Monitoring Form, which has evolved from the 12 tips for mental toughness first outlined in *Mental Toughness Training for Sports*.

This form is typically filled out by both the player and the coach following a match. It's best to wait a few hours—perhaps three or four, perhaps until the following day—for the player's head to clear before trying this exercise. At the Bollettieri Academy, if the child's match has been videotaped, the tape is often run before the form's done. We recommend that two forms be filled out for a player's match: one by the child and one by someone who watched the match —ideally the coach, but if not, then the parent, or another adult. Then the player's and observer's forms can be reviewed to see what the child's strengths and weaknesses were during the match.

The intention of this form, and the answers it provides, is simply to give the player useful feedback. Parents should not use this form as a way to criticize, for that will lead to counterproductive overinvolvement.

Still another useful tool for parents, players, and coaches is the Competitive Adjective Profile, a form designed to measure the traits associated with successful competitors. Here again we recommend that each member of the junior team —parent, player, and coach—fill out this form. Comparing the results of all of them, a coach can create a composite that indicates both strengths and weaknesses. The chart is scored from 1 to 10, from negative to positive. Obviously the higher the score is, the greater is the chance that a player has the characteristics associated with mental toughness.

Two or three times a year is a reasonable frequency for this test. This shouldn't become a tool for criticism. Rather, it should be used as a means by which behavior goals can be established.

A useful tool for understanding emotional response tendencies under pressure is the Emotional Response Inventory. This five-situation questionnaire posits competitive scenarios and asks the player to rank the four possible emotional responses in the order they best apply to him or her. The four possibilities reflect the four different energy states inherent in competition: low negative (tanking); high negative (anger); low positive (choking); and high positive (the challenge response).

In each of the five situations posed on this form, the responses are listed in an order that reflects the energy states a player passes through. The first listed response is the tanking stage, the second anger, the third choking, and the fourth challenge. The player's responses to these situations provide one more point of discussion for parent, player, and coach and ought to be reviewed two or three times a year.

At the Nick Bollettieri Academy, it's been proved over and over again how important it is for parents to have a regular written exchange between them and the coach evaluating the player's motivation, any discipline needed, how much the child's improving, and what areas need developing. Much of this philosophy is being incorporated in the USTA's new player development program, further attesting to its usefulness.

This kind of correspondence gives the parent a chance to participate and discuss the child's competitive development without assuming or challenging the coach's role. It also makes the coach think more carefully about the child, knowing that he or she will be asked for such an evaluation. The various forms used in this book, evaluations, and a diary give the coach and the parent the means to structure those exchanges and the opportunity for the child—in a hands-on, personal way—to set the goals and pace of his or her own development.

But parents have to remember that they need to achieve the same kind of positive energy state that they want for their children. Alert, enthused, supportive, energetic, inspired—all these are adjectives that describe the parent with the Challenge Response. A parent with low positive energy, in contrast, is uninterested but positive, underinvolved, isn't excited about taking the child anywhere or encouraging the child to stay involved with the game. A parent with high negative energy tends to be angry, unhappy about their child's tennis, irritable, nervous, under pressure, and frustrated with all the demands of the game. These parents tend to get upset with officials, with playing times, with all sorts of things. And low negative energy parents are bored with the whole thing. They are tired of tennis and the tournament scene and contribute—as do high negative and low positive parents—to the child's stress.

The trained parent is the parent who maintains the high positive energy profile he or she expects in the child. The trained parent understands the challenge response and the methods required to achieve it. In the end, the trained parent is the successful parent.

On the answer sheet provided, place an X in one of the five spaces for each item. Place only one check for each item. Your choices are Almost Always, Often, Sometimes, Seldom, and Almost Never. Select the one that seems to best fit your interpretation of the item as it relates to you in your sport. Obviously, your response is simply an estimate. Try to be as open and honest as you can with yourself and respond to each item as it pertains to you now.

1. I see myself more of a loser than a winner as a competitor.

2. I get angry and frustrated during competition.

3. I become distracted and lose my focus during competition.

4. Before competition, I picture myself performing perfectly.

5. I am highly motivated to play my best.

6. I can keep strong positive emotion flowing during competition.

7. I am a positive thinker during competition.

8. I really believe in myself as a player.

9. I get nervous or afraid in competition.

10. It seems my mind starts racing 100 mph during critical moments of competition.

11. I mentally practice my physical skills.

12. The goals I've set for myself as a player keep me working hard.

13. I am able to enjoy competition.

14. My self-talk during competition is negative.

15. I can lose my confidence very quickly.

16. Mistakes get me feeling and thinking in a negative way.

17. I can clear interfering emotions quickly.

18. Thinking in pictures about my sport comes easy for me.

19. I don't have to be pushed to play or practice hard. I am my own best igniter.

20. I tend to get emotionally flat when things turn against me during play.

21.   I give 100 percent effort during play, no matter what.

22.   I can perform toward the upper range of my talent and skill.

23.   My muscles become overly tight during competitions.

24.   I get spacey during competition.

25.   I visualize working through tough situations prior to competition.

26.   I'm willing to give whatever it takes to reach my full potential as a player.

27.   I practice with high positive intensity.

28.   I can change negative moods into positive ones by controlling my thinking.

29.   I'm a mentally tough competitor.

30.   I get more aggressive and attacking as the pressure mounts.

31.   I find myself thinking of past mistakes or missed opportunities as I play.

32.   I use images during play that help me perform better.

33.   I get bored and burned out.

34.   I get challenged and inspired in tough situations.

35.   My coaches would say I have a good attitude.

36.   I project the outward image of a confident fighter.

37.   I can remain calm during competition.

38.   My concentration is easily broken.

39.   When I visualize myself playing, I can see and feel things vividly.

40.   I wake up in the morning and am really excited about playing and practicing.

41.   Playing this sport gives me a genuine sense of joy and fulfillment.

42.   I can turn crisis into opportunity.

Answer Sheet

Name _____

Date _____

	ALMOST ALWAYS	OFTEN	SOMETIMES	SELDOM	ALMOST NEVER
1.	_____	_____	_____	_____	_____
2.	_____	_____	_____	_____	_____
3.	_____	_____	_____	_____	_____
4.	_____	_____	_____	_____	_____
5.	_____	_____	_____	_____	_____
6.	_____	_____	_____	_____	_____
7.	_____	_____	_____	_____	_____
8.	_____	_____	_____	_____	_____
9.	_____	_____	_____	_____	_____
10.	_____	_____	_____	_____	_____
11.	_____	_____	_____	_____	_____
12.	_____	_____	_____	_____	_____
13.	_____	_____	_____	_____	_____
14.	_____	_____	_____	_____	_____
15.	_____	_____	_____	_____	_____
16.	_____	_____	_____	_____	_____
17.	_____	_____	_____	_____	_____
18.	_____	_____	_____	_____	_____
19.	_____	_____	_____	_____	_____
20.	_____	_____	_____	_____	_____
21.	_____	_____	_____	_____	_____
22.	_____	_____	_____	_____	_____
23.	_____	_____	_____	_____	_____
24.	_____	_____	_____	_____	_____
25.	_____	_____	_____	_____	_____
26.	_____	_____	_____	_____	_____
27.	_____	_____	_____	_____	_____
28.	_____	_____	_____	_____	_____
29.	_____	_____	_____	_____	_____
30.	_____	_____	_____	_____	_____
31.	_____	_____	_____	_____	_____
32.	_____	_____	_____	_____	_____

Answer Sheet

Name _____

Date _____

	ALMOST ALWAYS	OFTEN	SOMETIMES	SELDOM	ALMOST NEVER
33.	_____	_____	_____	_____	_____
34.	_____	_____	_____	_____	_____
35.	_____	_____	_____	_____	_____
36.	_____	_____	_____	_____	_____
37.	_____	_____	_____	_____	_____
38.	_____	_____	_____	_____	_____
39.	_____	_____	_____	_____	_____
40.	_____	_____	_____	_____	_____
41.	_____	_____	_____	_____	_____
42.	_____	_____	_____	_____	_____

Summary Sheet

Name _____

Date _____

SELF-CONFIDENCE	NEGATIVE ENERGY CONTROL	ATTENTION CONTROL	VISUAL AND IMAGERY CONTROL	MOTIVATIONAL LEVEL	POSITIVE ENERGY CONTROL	ATTITUDE CONTROL
1 _____	2 _____	3 _____	4 _____	5 _____	6 _____	7 _____
8 _____	9 _____	10 _____	11 _____	12 _____	13 _____	14 _____
15 _____	16 _____	17 _____	18 _____	19 _____	20 _____	21 _____
22 _____	23 _____	24 _____	25 _____	26 _____	27 _____	28 _____
29 _____	30 _____	31 _____	32 _____	33 _____	34 _____	35 _____
36 _____	37 _____	38 _____	39 _____	40 _____	41 _____	42 _____
_____	_____	_____	_____	_____	_____	_____

```
30 ─┤
    │
25 ─┤
    │
20 ─┤
    │
15 ─┤
    │
10 ─┤
    │
 5 ─┤
    │
 0 ─┤
    └──────────────────────────────────────────────────────────
      SELF-    NEGATIVE   ATTEN-   VISUAL    MOTIVA-  POSITIVE   ATTITUDE
      CONFI-   ENERGY     TION     AND       TIONAL   ENERGY     CONTROL
      DENCE    CONTROL    CONTROL  IMAGERY   LEVEL    CONTROL
                                   CONTROL
```

During Play	EXCELLENT				POOR
Eyes controlled	1	2	3	4	5
Rituals Serve	1	2	3	4	5
Serve return	1	2	3	4	5
Winning pace	1	2	3	4	5
Breathing During points	1	2	3	4	5
Between points	1	2	3	4	5
Projected high positive intensity	1	2	3	4	5
Projected relaxation and calmness	1	2	3	4	5
Management of mistakes	1	2	3	4	5
Projected confident fighter image	1	2	3	4	5
Negative self-talk	1	2	3	4	5
Projected positive attitude	1	2	3	4	5
Projected "I love the battle"	1	2	3	4	5
Racket up ("I'm up")	1	2	3	4	5

During Play	**EXCELLENT**				**POOR**
Eyes controlled	1	2	3	4	5
Rituals Serve	1	2	3	4	5
Serve return	1	2	3	4	5
Winning pace	1	2	3	4	5
Breathing During points	1	2	3	4	5
Between points	1	2	3	4	5
Projected high positive intensity	1	2	3	4	5
Projected relaxation and calmness	1	2	3	4	5
Management of mistakes	1	2	3	4	5
Projected confident fighter image	1	2	3	4	5
Negative self-talk	1	2	3	4	5
Projected positive attitude	1	2	3	4	5
Projected "I love the battle"	1	2	3	4	5
Racket up ("I'm up")	1	2	3	4	5

Read each of the following situations carefully. Rank each of the four emotional responses beneath each situation according to how you would likely respond emotionally based on how you have responded in the past to similar problem situations. Rank 1 if that would be your most likely emotional response, 2 for your second most likely response, 3 for third most likely, and 4 for least likely.

Situation 1:
You've told your dad not to come and watch because you never play as well when he's there. He's very hard on you when you lose or don't play well.

RANK

Deliberately not play your best so your dad won't come next time.   _____

Get angry and upset during play because he promised he wouldn't come.   _____

Probably get more nervous because he never likes the way you play.   _____

Give your dad a dirty look but attempt to play well anyway. You will chew your dad
out for coming when the match is over.   _____

Situation 2:
Things are going badly, and it looks as if you're going to lose to someone you never should lose to. You are the better player by far, but you're not playing well.

RANK

Start acting as if you don't care and stop trying as hard.   _____

Get madder and madder because you're playing so badly and you don't want to lose
to this person.   _____

Get very nervous and embarrassed that you're losing to someone so bad.   _____

Continue fighting as hard as you can until it's over. People watching couldn't tell
whether you're winning or losing by the way you look. You look the same.   _____

Situation 3:
Your opponent has clearly cheated you out of several important points. You have requested a linesman twice and were told no one is available. You must continue to call your own lines.

RANK

If he needs to win that bad he can have it! I'm never playing this tournament again. I can't believe they have no one to call lines. What a joke!

_____

Who does this jerk think he is! I'm gonna get even. People who resort to cheating to win make me furious.

_____

I can't play. Every time I hit a ball, I'm afraid he'll call it out. I can't help but push.

_____

There's no way this turkey is going to cheat me out of this match. If I have to, I'll stay out here all day and hit 1,000 balls down the middle.

_____

Situation 4:
You're playing very poorly and about to lose to someone you can't stand who is also below you in ranking. How would you likely appear from a spectator's perspective?

RANK

Dragging, low energy, sagging shoulders

_____

Angry, upset, mad

_____

Positive but nervous

_____

Fighting, strong, and confident in spite of the problems

_____

Situation 5:
You don't feel like playing. You have a headache, and your ankle is sore. You would really rather not play, but you are not hurting enough to pull out.

RANK

You would try hard at the beginning, but if things went badly, you would not try as hard.

_____

When things start to go badly, you get upset with yourself for playing. You should have stayed home.

_____

When things start going badly, you start feeling afraid you won't win.

_____

When things start going badly, you will probably keep on trying the best you can and just hope things will get better.

_____

COMPETITIVE ADJECTIVE PROFILE

Name ________________________________

Completed by ________________________________

Date ________________________________

	BOLD	EVEN TEMPERED	COMPETITIVE	SELF-RELIANT	COMMITTED	AGGRESSIVE	CONFIDENT	PATIENT	DISCIPLINED	OPTIMISTIC	RESPONSIBLE	REALISTIC	CHALLENGED	COACHABLE	STABLE	MATURE	MOTIVATED	RELIABLE	PROBLEM SOLVER	TEAM PLAYER	TAKES RISKS	CONSISTENT	SCORE
10	•	•	•	•	•	•	•	•	•	•	•	•	•	•	•	•	•	•	•	•	•	•	______
9	•	•	•	•	•	•	•	•	•	•	•	•	•	•	•	•	•	•	•	•	•	•	______
8	•	•	•	•	•	•	•	•	•	•	•	•	•	•	•	•	•	•	•	•	•	•	______
7	•	•	•	•	•	•	•	•	•	•	•	•	•	•	•	•	•	•	•	•	•	•	______
6	•	•	•	•	•	•	•	•	•	•	•	•	•	•	•	•	•	•	•	•	•	•	______
5	•	•	•	•	•	•	•	•	•	•	•	•	•	•	•	•	•	•	•	•	•	•	______
4	•	•	•	•	•	•	•	•	•	•	•	•	•	•	•	•	•	•	•	•	•	•	______
3	•	•	•	•	•	•	•	•	•	•	•	•	•	•	•	•	•	•	•	•	•	•	______
2	•	•	•	•	•	•	•	•	•	•	•	•	•	•	•	•	•	•	•	•	•	•	______
1	•	•	•	•	•	•	•	•	•	•	•	•	•	•	•	•	•	•	•	•	•	•	______
	FEARFUL	MOODY	NON-COMPETITIVE	DEPENDENT	UNCOMMITTED	PASSIVE	INSECURE	IMPATIENT	UNDISCIPLINED	PESSIMISTIC	IRRESPONSIBLE	UNREALISTIC	FRIGHTENED	UNCOACHABLE	UNSTABLE	IMMATURE	UNMOTIVATED	UNRELIABLE	POOR PROBLEM SOLVER	TEAM PLAYER—POOR	UNWILLING TO TAKE RISKS	INCONSISTENT	______ TOTAL SCORE

COMPETITIVE ADJECTIVE PROFILE

Name _____
Completed by _____
Date _____

	BOLD	EVEN TEMPERED	COMPETITIVE	SELF-RELIANT	COMMITTED	AGGRESSIVE	CONFIDENT	PATIENT	DISCIPLINED	OPTIMISTIC	RESPONSIBLE	REALISTIC	CHALLENGED	COACHABLE	STABLE	MATURE	MOTIVATED	RELIABLE	PROBLEM SOLVER	TEAM PLAYER	TAKES RISKS	CONSISTENT	SCORE
10	·	·	·	·	·	·	·	·	·	·	·	·	·	·	·	·	·	·	·	·	·	·	___
9	·	·	·	·	·	·	·	·	·	·	·	·	·	·	·	·	·	·	·	·	·	·	___
8	·	·	·	·	·	·	·	·	·	·	·	·	·	·	·	·	·	·	·	·	·	·	___
7	·	·	·	·	·	·	·	·	·	·	·	·	·	·	·	·	·	·	·	·	·	·	___
6	·	·	·	·	·	·	·	·	·	·	·	·	·	·	·	·	·	·	·	·	·	·	___
5	·	·	·	·	·	·	·	·	·	·	·	·	·	·	·	·	·	·	·	·	·	·	___
4	·	·	·	·	·	·	·	·	·	·	·	·	·	·	·	·	·	·	·	·	·	·	___
3	·	·	·	·	·	·	·	·	·	·	·	·	·	·	·	·	·	·	·	·	·	·	___
2	·	·	·	·	·	·	·	·	·	·	·	·	·	·	·	·	·	·	·	·	·	·	___
1	·	·	·	·	·	·	·	·	·	·	·	·	·	·	·	·	·	·	·	·	·	·	___

FEARFUL, MOODY, NON-COMPETITIVE, DEPENDENT, UNCOMMITTED, PASSIVE, INSECURE, IMPATIENT, UNDISCIPLINED, PESSIMISTIC, IRRESPONSIBLE, UNREALISTIC, FRIGHTENED, UNCOACHABLE, UNSTABLE, IMMATURE, UNMOTIVATED, UNRELIABLE, POOR PROBLEM SOLVER, TEAM PLAYER—POOR, UNWILLING TO TAKE RISKS, INCONSISTENT

TOTAL SCORE

Name _____

Completed by _____

Date _____

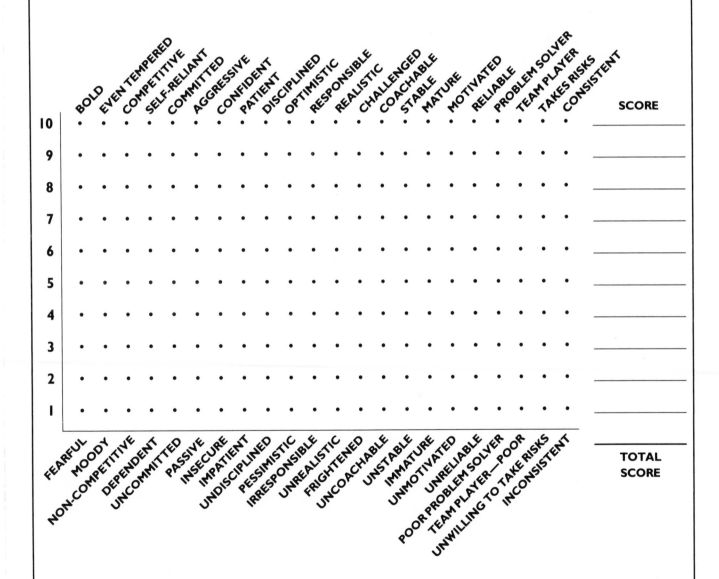

	BOLD	EVEN TEMPERED	COMPETITIVE	SELF-RELIANT	COMMITTED	AGGRESSIVE	CONFIDENT	PATIENT	DISCIPLINED	OPTIMISTIC	RESPONSIBLE	REALISTIC	CHALLENGED	COACHABLE	STABLE	MATURE	MOTIVATED	RELIABLE	PROBLEM SOLVER	TEAM PLAYER	TAKES RISKS	CONSISTENT	SCORE
10	•	•	•	•	•	•	•	•	•	•	•	•	•	•	•	•	•	•	•	•	•	•	_____
9	•	•	•	•	•	•	•	•	•	•	•	•	•	•	•	•	•	•	•	•	•	•	_____
8	•	•	•	•	•	•	•	•	•	•	•	•	•	•	•	•	•	•	•	•	•	•	_____
7	•	•	•	•	•	•	•	•	•	•	•	•	•	•	•	•	•	•	•	•	•	•	_____
6	•	•	•	•	•	•	•	•	•	•	•	•	•	•	•	•	•	•	•	•	•	•	_____
5	•	•	•	•	•	•	•	•	•	•	•	•	•	•	•	•	•	•	•	•	•	•	_____
4	•	•	•	•	•	•	•	•	•	•	•	•	•	•	•	•	•	•	•	•	•	•	_____
3	•	•	•	•	•	•	•	•	•	•	•	•	•	•	•	•	•	•	•	•	•	•	_____
2	•	•	•	•	•	•	•	•	•	•	•	•	•	•	•	•	•	•	•	•	•	•	_____
1	•	•	•	•	•	•	•	•	•	•	•	•	•	•	•	•	•	•	•	•	•	•	_____

FEARFUL MOODY NON-COMPETITIVE DEPENDENT UNCOMMITTED PASSIVE INSECURE IMPATIENT UNDISCIPLINED PESSIMISTIC IRRESPONSIBLE UNREALISTIC FRIGHTENED UNCOACHABLE UNSTABLE IMMATURE UNMOTIVATED UNRELIABLE POOR PROBLEM SOLVER TEAM PLAYER—POOR UNWILLING TO TAKE RISKS INCONSISTENT

TOTAL SCORE _____

Name _____
Completed by _____
Date _____

	BOLD	EVEN TEMPERED	COMPETITIVE	SELF-RELIANT	COMMITTED	AGGRESSIVE	CONFIDENT	PATIENT	DISCIPLINED	OPTIMISTIC	RESPONSIBLE	REALISTIC	CHALLENGED	COACHABLE	STABLE	MATURE	MOTIVATED	RELIABLE	PROBLEM SOLVER	TEAM PLAYER	TAKES RISKS	CONSISTENT	SCORE
10	·	·	·	·	·	·	·	·	·	·	·	·	·	·	·	·	·	·	·	·	·	·	_____
9	·	·	·	·	·	·	·	·	·	·	·	·	·	·	·	·	·	·	·	·	·	·	_____
8	·	·	·	·	·	·	·	·	·	·	·	·	·	·	·	·	·	·	·	·	·	·	_____
7	·	·	·	·	·	·	·	·	·	·	·	·	·	·	·	·	·	·	·	·	·	·	_____
6	·	·	·	·	·	·	·	·	·	·	·	·	·	·	·	·	·	·	·	·	·	·	_____
5	·	·	·	·	·	·	·	·	·	·	·	·	·	·	·	·	·	·	·	·	·	·	_____
4	·	·	·	·	·	·	·	·	·	·	·	·	·	·	·	·	·	·	·	·	·	·	_____
3	·	·	·	·	·	·	·	·	·	·	·	·	·	·	·	·	·	·	·	·	·	·	_____
2	·	·	·	·	·	·	·	·	·	·	·	·	·	·	·	·	·	·	·	·	·	·	_____
1	·	·	·	·	·	·	·	·	·	·	·	·	·	·	·	·	·	·	·	·	·	·	_____
	FEARFUL	MOODY	NON-COMPETITIVE	DEPENDENT	UNCOMMITTED	PASSIVE	INSECURE	IMPATIENT	UNDISCIPLINED	PESSIMISTIC	IRRESPONSIBLE	UNREALISTIC	FRIGHTENED	UNCOACHABLE	UNSTABLE	IMMATURE	UNMOTIVATED	UNRELIABLE	POOR PROBLEM SOLVER	TEAM PLAYER—POOR	UNWILLING TO TAKE RISKS	INCONSISTENT	TOTAL SCORE